MW00437127

"This book is a masterfι
church historian. We see
Calvin the man. His min
work. A must read."
—R. C. SPROUL, Chairman and President,
Ligonier Ministries, Lake Mary, Florida

"*John Calvin: Pilgrim and Pastor* will surely rank among the best
introductions to the life and thought of one of the church's greatest theologians. It offers a rich tapestry woven from both Calvin's
life-story and his profound biblical theology. Here we meet the real
Calvin—strikingly apostolic in his constant preaching, his lecturing, his
authorship of many erudite volumes and a vast correspondence, and
his deep care for the many needs of his flock—while himself in constant physical sickness. It is a remarkable story. Dr. Robert Godfrey's
mature scholarship, enthusiasm for his subject, and easy style bring
Calvin to life for the twenty-first-century reader. Here is a rare work
indeed, making it easy to see why the great Genevan Reformer was
such an inspiration to those who knew and loved him."
—SINCLAIR B. FERGUSON, Senior Minister,
First Presbyterian Church, Columbia, South Carolina

"There are good books on Calvin's doctrine, his life, his piety, and
his influence in the modern world. However, this book stands out as
a marvelous integration of all three. More than accessible, this book
is interesting even for those who know nothing about Calvin or his
significant labors. It would be dishonest to deny that this book is
written by an admirer of Calvin, but as a veteran church historian,
Professor Godfrey places the reformer in his context and does not hide
his blemishes. I owe a great deal of my own formative understanding
of Calvin to Robert Godfrey and hope for a wide readership of this
important book."
—MICHAEL S. HORTON, J. Gresham Machen
Professor of Systematic Theology and Apologetics,
Westminster Seminary California

"Bob Godfrey has long been known as doing the unimaginable and has once again lived up to his reputation. His work on Calvin offers not only an accessible history of the man and his work, and an assessment of his influence, but also allows Calvin to be seen through his own words and offers an opportunity for another generation to appreciate the vastness of his genius. Combining excellent scholarship with an accessible style, Dr. Godfrey has once again placed the church in his debt as he resurrects the character from the caricature in which Calvin is so often buried."

—ROBERT M. NORRIS, Pastor, Fourth Presbyterian Church, Bethesda, Maryland

"This book is arguably the best introduction to the life and ministry of John Calvin by one of the Reformed world's best interpreters of the Reformation. For anyone wondering what the fuss is over the 500th anniversary of Calvin's birth, this is the place to start."

—D. G. HART, author of *The Lost Soul of American Protestantism* and *Defending the Faith: J. Gresham Machen and the Crisis of Conservative Protestantism in Modern America*

JOHN CALVIN

PILGRIM AND PASTOR

W. ROBERT GODFREY

CROSSWAY BOOKS

WHEATON, ILLINOIS

John Calvin: Pilgrim and Pastor

Copyright © 2009 by W. Robert Godfrey

Published by Crossway Books
   a publishing ministry of Good News Publishers
   1300 Crescent Street
   Wheaton, Illinois 60187

Cover design: Tobias' Outerwear for Books

First printing, 2009

Printed in the United States of America

Unless otherwise indicated, Scripture quotations are taken from the ESV® Bible (*The Holy Bible: English Standard Version*®). Copyright © 2001 by Crossway Bibles, a publishing ministry of Good News Publishers. Used by permission. All rights reserved.

Scripture quotations marked NASB are from *The New American Standard Bible.*® Copyright © The Lockman Foundation 1960, 1962, 1963, 1968, 1971, 1972, 1973, 1975, 1977, 1995. Used by permission.

ISBN PDF: 978-1-4335-1195-0

ISBN Mobipocket: 978-1-4335-1196-7

Library of Congress Cataloging-in-Publication Data
Godfrey, W. Robert.
 John Calvin : pilgrim and pastor / W. Robert Godfrey.
  p. cm.
 Includes bibliographical references and index.
 ISBN 978-1-4335-0132-6 (tpb)
 1. Calvin, Jean, 1509–1564. I. Title
BX9418.G585 2009
284'.2092—dc22   2008047480

VP		19	18	17	16	15	14	13	12	11	10	09
15	14	13	12	11	10	9	8	7	6	5	4	3	2

CONTENTS

Introduction: The Importance of Calvin   7

PILGRIM

1   Calvin in Strassburg   13

2   The Young Calvin   23

3   Calvin's First Ministry in Geneva   35

4   Exiled to Strassburg   43

PASTOR

5   The Call Back to Geneva   57

6   The Church and Worship   69

7   The Church and the Sacraments   87

8   The Church and Predestination   113

9   The Church, the City, and the Schools   129

10   Calvin as Pastoral Counselor   139

11   Calvin and the *Institutes*   167

Conclusion: The Unmarked Grave   193

General Index   201

INTRODUCTION:
THE IMPORTANCE OF CALVIN

July 10, 2009 marks the five-hundredth anniversary of the birth of John Calvin (1509–1564). Today for many people the name of Calvin is known only in a vague sense and has become a label for attitudes that are negative, judgmental, and joyless. Historians, by contrast, know that John Calvin was one of the most remarkable men who lived in the last five hundred years and that his influence on the development of the modern western world has been immense. Calvin and Calvinism have been linked to the rise of such diverse phenomena as democracy, capitalism, and modern science. Theologians and biblical scholars know him as a writer in theology and biblical studies whose work must still be carefully considered today. Church historians remember him as the principal theologian of Reformed Christianity—an expression of the Christian faith that over four and a half centuries has attracted millions of adherents in countries throughout the world. He was indeed a leader and writer whose work affected the life and worship of countless congregations and has inspired thousands of pastors, theologians, and biblical scholars.

The life and work of John Calvin have always been controversial as well as influential. Some have loved him, and some have hated him. All would agree that he was a man with a brilliant mind and a powerful will who had a profound impact on the development of western civilization. But was that impact positive or negative?

His critics have been many. In his own day they sometimes railed at him—naming their dogs after him—and sometimes laughed at him, some suggesting that his wife died of boredom. Some modern critics have been savage. Will Durant wrote, ". . . we shall always find it hard to love the man who darkened the human soul with the most absurd and blasphemous conception of God in all the long and honored history of nonsense."[1]

On the positive side, Calvin's friend and colleague Theodore Beza (1519–1605) wrote a brief biography of Calvin to answer the critics of his day. Beza's admiring work breathes a spirit of affection and warmth, observing that "in the common inter-course of life, there was no man who was more pleasant."[2] He concluded his biography, "Having been a spectator of his conduct for sixteen years . . . I can now declare, that in him all men may see a most beautiful example of the Christian character, an exam-ple which it is as easy to slander as it is difficult to imitate."[3]

The real Calvin was not in the first place a man who lived to influence future generations. Rather he was a spiritual pilgrim finding anew the apostolic Christianity expressed in the Bible and serving as a faithful minister of that Word in the church of his day. The influence that Calvin would have regarded as most important was as a purifier of the Christian religion and a reformer of the church for his day. The essential Calvin was a pilgrim and pastor. From that reality all his influence flowed.

Calvin saw the importance of his life as a pastor in his own day and did not focus on his influence in years to come. When his friend William Farel urged him to publish his study of Genesis, he replied, "As to my observations on Genesis, if the Lord shall grant me longer life and leisure, perhaps I will set myself about that work, although I do not expect to have many hearers. This is my especial end and aim, to serve my generation; and for the rest, if, in my present calling, an occasional opportunity offers itself, I shall endeavor to improve it for those who come after us. I have a mind to set about writing several things, but as my wife

---

[1]Will Durant, *The Reformation (The Story of Civilization, Part VI)*, (New York: Simon & Schuster, 1957), 490.
[2]Theodore Beza, *The Life of John Calvin*, in *Selected Works of John Calvin*, Vol. 1, ed. H. Beveridge and J. Bonnet (Grand Rapids, MI: Baker, 1983), xcvii.
[3]Beza, in ibid., c.

is now in ill health, not without danger, my attention is otherwise engaged."[4]

In his own day he was above all else a pastor who had a passion for the gospel of Christ. It was that gospel and that passion that ultimately moved millions. He communicated faith, hope, and confidence in God. A Roman Catholic Spanish soldier in the Netherlands observed some years after Calvin's death that he would rather face a whole army than one Calvinist convinced he was doing the will of God. Reformed Christianity was not a mild and innocuous religion. It was moving and powerful.

This book is an introduction to the life and thought of John Calvin. It aims at communicating Calvin's passion and faith through extensive quotations from his works so that something of the force and eloquence of his language can be experienced by the reader.[5] He moved millions not through the power of his personality but through the power of his biblical ideas and words. This book focuses on the essential Calvin, a man who lived out his Christian faith as a pilgrim and a pastor.

[4]John Calvin, "Letters," July 28, 1542, in *Selected Works of John Calvin*, Vol. 4, ed. H. Beveridge and J. Bonnet (Grand Rapids, MI: Baker, 1983), 339.
[5]In order to make Calvin's eloquence clearer to the contemporary reader, quotations from his commentaries and treatises have often been modernized.

PILGRIM

Calvin in Strassburg

On July 10, 1539 John Calvin reached his thirtieth birthday. In many ways his future did not seem very promising. He had shown his intelligence and scholarship in two books he had written, but his life had been very troubled. He had fled from his native France after his conversion to the Protestant faith and had ended up in the Swiss city of Geneva. After less than two years of pastoral service there, he was exiled from Geneva along with other ministers because of their insistence on moral discipline in the church. A discouraged and embittered Calvin traveled to Strassburg, an independent, German-speaking city-state in the Holy Roman Empire near the border with France. There he became the pastor of a small congregation of a few hundred French refugees. Calvin's years in Strassburg were a relief for him as he enjoyed a less conspicuous life than he'd had in Geneva, pastoring, studying, and writing. At the age of thirty, in his second exile, his body was beginning to show its tendency for weakness and illness. (In fact he had less than twenty-five years to live.) No one could have predicted that from these modest and uncertain circumstances Calvin would rise to be one of the most influential men of his age and of the modern era.

Yet 1539 was a turning point for Calvin. In that year he completed the first of his commentaries on books of the Bible, a commentary on Paul's letter to the Romans. He also published the first major revision of his *Institutes of the Christian Religion*, moving it from being an introduction to basic Christianity toward being a full systematic theology. Both of these works pointed to his developing interests and insights. But a third work that he wrote that year is the most important as an introduction to the life and thought of Calvin. This work is his famous treatise known as "Reply to Sadoleto."

Calvin's treatise was a response to a sharp attack on the Reformation written by Jacopo Sadoleto. Sadoleto was a bishop and cardinal of the Roman Catholic Church and a distinguished scholar. After hearing of the exile of Calvin and other pastors, he wrote to the Genevans in 1538 urging them to return to the old church. While the Genevan authorities did not regard Sadoleto's letter as a real threat to the Protestant establishment in Geneva, they did want a strong and effective response written to it. After careful consideration they finally realized that their former pastor Calvin, whom they had exiled, was the best equipped to write the answer they wanted.

Calvin must have received their request with some amusement and satisfaction. Their recognition that they needed him surely made Calvin feel vindicated. He saw the importance of the task and quickly set to work writing his "Reply to Sadoleto." He completed the treatise in six days. Theodore Beza wrote that the work was full of "truth and eloquence."[1] More recent scholars have evaluated the treatise as one of the most powerful defenses of the Reformation ever written.

Calvin's "Reply to Sadoleto" is important for more than its brilliant defense of Reformed Christianity. It is also a window into Calvin's soul. Calvin was usually very reticent to write much about himself, but in this work there is a remarkable personal quality that reveals a great deal about him.

By nature Calvin was a very private person. In few of his works does he write about himself. Even in his letters he does not become introspective or discuss the events of his personal life in much detail. But in "Reply to Sadoleto" he reveals indirectly a

---

[1]Theodore Beza, *The Life of John Calvin*, in *Selected Works of John Calvin*, Vol. 1, ed. H. Beveridge and J. Bonnet (Grand Rapids, MI: Baker, 1983), xxxv.

good deal of his own experience of the Reformation and the key motivations of his life. These experiences and convictions of his life are also key elements of the religion he taught as a pastor.

The character of Sadoleto's appeal to the Genevans provided several incentives for Calvin to show something of his own experience in his reply. First, Sadoleto made a very personal attack on Calvin and the other ministers, saying that they had been motivated in their reforming work only by a desire for fame and money. Second, Sadoleto argued that only the Roman Catholic Church possessed truth, certainty, and salvation—issues of deep personal significance for Calvin. Third, Sadoleto had created several prayers in his treatise that he had put in the mouths of an imagined person to illustrate some of the points he was making. These prayers written in the first person evoked from Calvin a response written in the same language. This literary device was well known to Calvin who was acquainted with it from the writings of Quintilian, the ancient teacher of rhetoric, and had been commented on by Calvin in his early commentary on Seneca:

> . . . *prosopopoeia,* by which it is pretended that the emperor is talking with himself, and so to speak entering into meditation. . . . And these words are more appealing through a pretended person, than if conceived as from the person of the author. So Quintilian [*Institutes of Oratory*, 9.2.29] teaches. For they are effective to arouse the reader, to stir feelings, to vary the discourse. Some call this figure not *prosopopoeia* but *ethopoea, because the former invents persons who nowhere exist, whereas the latter fits these words to definite* persons.[2]

Calvin was not being intentionally autobiographical with these prayers, but they inevitably reflected something of his own personal experience of spiritual things.

Calvin's "Reply" began with a vigorous rejection of the idea that he was motivated by a desire for fame or money. He could more easily have found those in the Church of Rome. What

---

[2]John Calvin, *Commentary on Seneca's De Clementia*, trans. F.L. Battles and A.M. Hugo (Leiden: E.J. Brill, 1969), 29.

motivated him, he insisted, above all was a concern for the glory of God. Where Sadoleto had declared that the Christian should first be concerned for his own salvation, Calvin maintained that the Christian must first be focused on God and his glory: "It is not very sound theology to confine a man's thoughts so much to himself, and not to set before him, as the prime motive of his existence, zeal to show forth the glory of God. For we are born first of all for God, and not for ourselves."[3] Calvin always intended his life and thought to be God-centered.

For Calvin, once the Christian saw the glory of God as central, then a proper discussion of salvation could follow. Only when we see God as truly glorious can we see the true nature of salvation and its importance. He wrote to Sadoleto, ". . . you have a theology that is too lazy, as is almost always the case with those who have had no experience in serious struggles of conscience."[4] Laziness and self-indulgence are not the path to true theology. Calvin believed that such attitudes had dominated the old church in which he had been raised and produced a church life filled with formalism, indifference, and superstition.

Calvin's criticism of Sadoleto at this point certainly implied that he himself had had serious struggles of conscience. What kinds of struggles? We can see echoes of those experiences in Calvin's discussions of justification. He had struggled with the great question of how to be right with God. Calvin stressed that a correct understanding of justification was fundamental. He wrote to Sadoleto that justification was "the first and keenest subject of controversy between us."[5]

Calvin presents his thought on justification in his "Reply" in terms of several steps. The first was self-examination. The sinner must come to recognize his own plight: "First, we tell a man to begin by examining himself. He must not do this in a superficial or perfunctory way, but must call his conscience before the

[3]John Calvin, "Reply to Sadoleto," *Selected Works of John Calvin*, Vol. 1, ed. H. Beveridge and J. Bonnet (Grand Rapids, MI: Baker, 1983), 33, translation altered.
[4]Ibid., 52, translation altered.
[5]Ibid., 41.

judgment seat of God. When he is sufficiently convinced of his iniquity, then he must reflect on the strictness of the judgment pronounced on all sinners. When thus confronted and amazed at his misery, then he prostrates and humbles himself before God. He casts away all self-confidence and groans as if given up for final destruction."[6] The conscience of the sinner must come to see profoundly his lostness and helplessness. Calvin made this same point in his *Institutes*: ". . . no man can descend into himself and seriously consider his own character, without perceiving that God is angry with him and hostile to him."[7]

This theme of very serious and searching self-examination was not an incidental matter for Calvin. Rather it was absolutely central to Reformation theology and spirituality. In many ways the Reformation was born out of the sense of the hopelessness and spiritual powerlessness of sinners. For Calvin the complete lostness of man was not only a teaching of the Bible and of all sound theology since the days of the church father Augustine (354–430)—it was also part of his own experience. Scattered throughout the "Reply" are indications that Calvin had personally struggled with his own sin and the terrible judgment that awaited him apart from Christ.

Calvin preserved something of this struggle before coming to faith in his final edition of the *Institutes* in the very first section of the first chapter: ". . . every one, therefore, must be so impressed with a consciousness of his own unhappiness as to arrive at some knowledge of God. Thus a sense of our own ignorance, vanity, infirmity, depravity, and corruption, leads us to perceive and acknowledge that in the Lord alone are to be found true wisdom, solid strength, perfect goodness, and unspotted righteousness."[8]

For example, in the "Reply" Calvin elaborates on this theme of struggle in one of the prayers he puts in the mouth of his average Christian: "I expected a future resurrection, but hated to think of

---

[6]Ibid., translation altered.
[7]John Calvin, *Institutes of the Christian Religion*, trans. John Allen (Philadelphia: Presbyterian Board of Christian Education, 1816), II, 16, 1.
[8]Ibid., I, 1, 1, altered.

it, since it would be a most dreadful event. And this feeling not only had dominion over me in private, but had its origin in the doctrine that was then everywhere delivered to the people by their Christian teachers."[9] Further the prayer speaks of efforts to satisfy God with works of righteousness: "When, however, I had performed all these things, though I had some intervals of quiet, I was still far-off from true peace of conscience; for, whenever I descended into myself, or raised my mind to you, O God, extreme terror seized me—terror which no expiations or satisfactions could cure. And the more closely I examined myself, the sharper the stings with which my conscience was pricked, so that the only solace which remained to me was to delude myself by forgetfulness."[10]

Although these prayers are not strictly autobiographical, they are so intense and personal that they must reflect something of Calvin's experiences in his own conversion only six or seven years earlier. He had come to see for himself his desperate condition and had come to see it as essential for all sound theology and religious experience.

To Sadoleto Calvin insisted that after this self-knowledge the next necessity was a knowledge of God's way of salvation. The sinner could hope only in God and his work since the work of man is utterly futile. Again Calvin puts words in the mouth of his representative Christian: "I was exceedingly alarmed at the misery into which I had fallen, and much more alarmed at the eternal death that threatened me. As in duty bound, I made it my first business to find your way, condemning my past life, but with groans and tears."[11] That way of God is the way of Christ. A knowledge of the work of Christ as God's way of salvation is the second step of justification. Calvin, writing as a pastor and teacher, said, "Then we show that the only haven of safety is in the mercy of God, as shown in Christ. In him every part of our salvation is complete."[12]

---

[9]Calvin, "Reply to Sadoleto," 61, translation altered.
[10]Ibid., 62, translation altered.
[11]Ibid., 64, translation altered.
[12]Ibid., 42, translation altered.

For Calvin, Christ displayed all the promises of God concerning the Savior who would fully bear the sins of his people on the cross and impute the saving benefits of his work to them. These promises brought salvation to the sinner when they were received through faith alone. Faith was the link between Christ and the sinner. "Paul, whenever he attributed to faith the power of justifying, restricted it to a free promise of the divine favor, and keeps it far removed from all works."[13] Faith rests alone in the promise of salvation in Jesus.

Calvin showed Sadoleto that the result of the faith that rests in the justifying work of Christ is great peace and assurance for the Christian. "He has nothing of Christ, then, who does not hold this basic principle, that it is God alone who enlightens our minds to perceive his truth, who seals it on our hearts by his Spirit and who by his sure witness confirms it to our conscience. This is, if I may so express it, that full and firm assurance commended by Paul."[14] Calvin stresses the "confident hope of salvation both commanded by your Word, and founded on it."[15] Struggles of conscience drove Calvin to faith in Christ, and that faith brought a settled assurance and confidence to his soul.

Calvin challenged not only Sadoleto's understanding of the way of salvation, but also of the final authority on matters of religion. They both knew that the issue of authority was foundational to the religious and doctrinal disputes of the Reformation era. For Sadoleto, sound doctrine came from the absolute teaching authority of the inerrant Roman Church. As part of that authority he claimed the Holy Spirit, the church, the universal councils, and his ancestors as the basis of the doctrine that he followed.

How did Calvin approach the issue of authority in answering Sadoleto? He began by recognizing the need for an absolute authority that stands above anything doubtful or human: "Christian faith must not be founded on human testimony, not

---

[13]Ibid., 42f., translation altered.
[14]Ibid., 53, translation altered.
[15]Ibid., 57, translation altered.

propped up by doubtful opinion, not resting on human authority, but graven on our hearts by the finger of the living God, so as not to be obliterated by any coloring of error."[16] Authority must be sought from God alone and the means that he uses.

For Calvin, Christians could only find this certain authority in the Scriptures. He fully embraced the *sola Scriptura* standard of the Reformation and eloquently presented it. The Word of God alone contains certain truth and clear direction for faith: "We hold that the Word of God alone lies beyond the sphere of our judgment." All other claims to authority must be evaluated by the Scriptures. He insisted that ". . . Fathers and Councils are of authority only in so far as they agree with the rule of the Word."[17] The Scriptures stand as the judge of the church and all human thought.

Calvin did not treat the authority of Scripture simply as a sparring point with Sadoleto. The Bible was at the heart of the life and experience of the Christian community. Calvin had personally wrestled with the question of authority. He was long attached to the authority of the church and only in his conversion accepted the authority of the Scriptures in all religious matters.

For Calvin, a faithful pastor could only nourish and develop the people of God with the Word. Calvin asked those who would call themselves pastors and teachers to examine themselves on this point: "I will only exhort these men to turn for once to themselves, and consider with what faithfulness they feed the Christian people, who cannot have any other food than the Word of their God."[18] Calvin lived his life as a pastor who sought to nourish and guide both himself and his flock with the Scriptures.

Calvin did not dismiss Sadoleto's concern for the authority of the church in a cavalier or individualistic fashion. He made clear that he loved the unity and harmony of the church. But that church must honor the Word of God above itself. "May ours be the humility which, beginning with the lowest, and paying

---

[16]Ibid., 53, translation altered.
[17]Ibid., 66, translation altered.
[18]Ibid., 65, translation altered.

respect to each in his degree, yields the highest honor and respect to the Church, in subordination, however, to Christ, the Church's head. May ours be the obedience which, while it disposes us to listen to our elders and superiors, tests all obedience by the Word of God. Last, may ours be the Church whose supreme care it is humbly and religiously to venerate the Word of God, and submit to its authority."[19] In this same vein, he presents a prayer: "My conscience told me how strong the zeal was with which I burned for the unity of your Church, provided your truth were made the bond of harmony."[20] The Word must be the power of life and peace within the church. True unity and peace are in the truth of the Scriptures.

Calvin acknowledged that asserting the authority of the Word was not a simple solution to all problems. The Word itself was sometimes misunderstood. But whatever the problem or difficulty, the Word was a better and clearer and safer guide than some supposed inerrancy in the church. He has the Christian in his "Reply" pray: ". . . the only thing I asked was that all controversies should be decided by your Word."[21]

For Calvin the Holy Spirit taught the truth of justification through the Scriptures in the church. Calvin's great concerns for justification, the Word of God, and the church were united and energized by his belief in the Holy Spirit. For this reason he reacted sharply to Sadoleto's improper appeal to the Spirit as a guide for the church apart from the Word. "The Spirit was promised not to reveal a new doctrine, but to impress the truth of the gospel on our minds. . . . And you, Sadoleto, by stumbling on the very threshold [of theology], have paid the penalty of that offense which you offered to the Holy Spirit when you separated him from the Word. . . . The Spirit goes before the Church, to enlighten her in understanding the Word, while the Word itself is like the Lydian stone [a touchstone], by which she tests all doctrines."[22]

---

[19] Ibid., 50, translation altered.
[20] Ibid., 60, translation altered.
[21] Ibid., translation altered.
[22] Ibid., 36ff., translation altered.

Only the Spirit could open the eyes of Christians, including leaders of the church, to the truth of God's Word.

Calvin's "Reply" in 1539 was shaped by his passion for the glory of God and by the peace with God that he had experienced in Christ after his recognition of the seriousness of his sin. He was convinced that only through the Bible and the work of the Holy Spirit had he come to know this peace in Christ. He was certain that the old church had gravely distorted the truth and needed thorough reform.

These certainties that guided the life and work of John Calvin developed out of his own experience. They met needs in his life that were theological but were also deeply personal. For him personally his struggles of conscience were relieved by the certainty of the gospel of grace. Theologically the certain church of the Middle Ages was replaced by the certain Scripture of the Reformation. These certainties to which Calvin had come gave him a clear focus amidst the anxieties and changes of his life. One scholar called Calvin "a singularly anxious man."[23] While such a statement may be somewhat exaggerated, Calvin did have anxieties that emerged both from his personal experiences and from the rapid changes that society was undergoing in the sixteenth century. In response to these anxieties Calvin found great certainties in religion reformed by the Bible. Those certainties brought a stability to his life that is reflected in the clarity of his thought and his great productivity as pastor and theologian. Calvin lived out the faith about which he had written to Sadoleto, a faith that was "that full and firm assurance commended by Paul, which leaves no room for doubt, and does not hesitate and waver among human arguments about which party to join. Rather it maintains its consistency though the whole world oppose it."[24]

---

[23]William J. Bouwsma, "The Quest for the Historical Calvin," *Archiv fuer Reformationsgeschichte*, 77 (1986), 53.
[24]Calvin, "Reply to Sadoleto," 53, translation altered.

THE YOUNG CALVIN

In his first twenty-six years Calvin developed from a provincial boy to a splendidly educated scholar. He changed from being a loyal son of the old church in Noyon to being a rootless Protestant on the move. He laid the foundations in his studies, faith, and early writings on which the rest of his life would be built.

DUTIFUL SON

John Calvin was born on July 10, 1509 in the city of Noyon in the kingdom of France. He was born into a world that still appeared traditionally medieval but like the rest of Europe was in fact experiencing an accelerated rate of change in many ways. The modern world was beginning to emerge in Europe, a world of changing patterns in social, economic, political, and intellectual life. The medieval ideal of a rather static Christian society dominated by a universal church and a universal empire was fading. The middle class, cities, and commerce were becoming more important in a world where nobles and peasants with their roots in rural agriculture were traditional. Nations and territories would weaken the ideal of a holy empire, and the Renaissance recovery of ancient Roman and Greek thought would begin to advance the importance of the individual, so characteristic of much modern thought.

These changes, however, were not very evident in Noyon in 1509. Noyon was a city about sixty miles north and slightly east of Paris in a region of France called Picardy. It was a small city of perhaps seven thousand inhabitants. Its life was dominated by the church and the bishop who resided there, Noyon being his episcopal seat. Aside from church matters, the city was primarily agricultural in outlook.

Calvin's family—the original name was Cauvin—had seen significant improvement in their fortunes in recent generations. Calvin's paternal grandfather had been a boatman and barrel-maker in the village of Pont l'Eveque near Noyon, a modest occupation and location. Calvin's father, Gerard, moved to the city of Noyon in 1481 and prospered there. He did important work for the legal and financial concerns of the church. He married Jeanne Le Franc, a reputed beauty whose father had been an innkeeper in Cambrai in the southern part of the Low Countries.

Gerard and Jeanne had several children. As was common in those days, some of the children died in infancy. Three boys reached maturity—Charles, John, and Antoine. Jeanne, about whom very little is known, died when John was about five years old. Gerard remarried, but almost nothing is known about his second wife except that she bore at least two daughters. Gerard was over fifty when John was born.

John Calvin's reticence to speak or write much about his personal life certainly extended to his parents and stepmother. We can reconstruct little about his family life. However, it is clear that he respected his father and was an obedient son. His father certainly recognized Calvin's talents as a student and provided a fine education for him. We also know that John remained close to his two brothers and at least one half-sister, Marie. They came to share his commitment to the Protestant faith and eventually joined him in exile in Geneva.

Gerard Calvin believed that the connections he had established in Noyon would profit his sons. He particularly believed that he could help them advance their fortunes through careers in the church. Charles became a priest (leaving the priesthood in 1537). Gerard secured for John when he was only eleven his first benefice. Such a benefice was a church appointment that carried with it some income but no responsibilities.

The young John Calvin formed friendships with the sons of the de Hangest family, which must have pleased his father very much. The de Hangest family was the local nobility; the bishop of Noyon was another member of this family. John was both personable and intellectually talented enough that the de Hangests encouraged this friendship. His father no doubt hoped that this relationship would significantly advance his son's future career.

From a modern perspective it may be tempting to look at these limited facts about the early life of Calvin and try to draw some conclusions about the development of Calvin psychologically. If Calvin lost his mother while quite young and was raised by a stepmother, did this make him anxious, shy, fearful? If Calvin had friends who were much wealthier and more powerful than he, did he feel inferior and resentful? Such questions may seem appropriate in our day but may be misleading for the sixteenth century. Many children in that time lost mothers to disease and complications arising from childbirth. They also frequently lost siblings. Children then were also raised in a world with strong notions of status and station. Living with differences of wealth and influence was common. Nothing about Calvin's youth was unusual for the time. In fact, Calvin's life was more privileged than most and was not particularly troubled. Calvin's relations with his father and siblings suggest a strong and positive family experience. His lifelong respect for members of the nobility seems in part to reflect his positive experience with the de Hangest family.

Around 1521 the young Calvin accompanied his friends in the de Hangest family to Paris to continue his education. He would have already begun his careful and thorough education in the Latin language in Noyon. This part of his education was the first part of the threefold way (*trivium*) of medieval education. The student began with grammar and then advanced to logic and rhetoric. Calvin was quick with his learning and would in time become a great stylist in both the Latin and French languages.

In Paris he apparently continued his study of Latin for a year and then began his studies in logic at the Collège de Montaigu of the University of Paris. What exactly Calvin studied there is unknown, but he would have received an education that was still traditionally medieval with lectures that were commentaries on notable books on logic. This course of study was designed to prepare young men like Calvin for the later study of theology. While some scholars have speculated about what specific theological influences from this time of study may have shaped Calvin's later thought, nothing can be known for sure.

Around 1526 Calvin was suddenly directed by his father to abandon his studies for the priesthood and to begin studies to become a lawyer. These studies he faithfully undertook at schools in Orléans and Bourges until 1531. While the reasons Gerard changed his plans for the future of his son are unknown, they may have reflected his own troubles with the church. Gerard was having problems with church authorities and on November 2, 1528 was excommunicated for failing to provide audited records for some of his financial dealings with the church.

Calvin's new studies not only provided him with legal knowledge that was useful to him later in life, they also sharpened his thinking. Furthermore, these studies enabled him to broaden his acquaintance with scholars of his day and led to his growing admiration of Renaissance learning. Bourges was a center of a new approach to studying the law. Here the Renaissance pursuit of ancient sources of western thought and of eloquent communication had affected the study of law. The new approach to learning clearly captivated Calvin.

AMBITIOUS SCHOLAR

The Renaissance was becoming an influential presence in France in the early sixteenth century. It attracted young men particularly for several reasons. In learning it gave them a sense of superiority to their elders. Aesthetically the writings of the ancient Romans and Greeks were much finer and more beautiful than the writings of the medievals. The Renaissance learning not only made men the masters of three languages (Latin, Greek, and Hebrew) but also taught them to write in an eloquent manner that became fashionable in many civic circles. This fashion meant that young men with a Renaissance education could often find desirable positions as secretaries to rich and influential people.

The finest of those educated in the new learning often became editors and commentators on some of the great writings of antiquity. The most celebrated of these scholars in northern Europe was Desiderius Erasmus who provided critical editions of such church fathers as Jerome and Augustine. Calvin, like many young men, sought to emulate the scholarly achievements of Erasmus.

On May 26, 1531 Gerard Calvin died in Noyon. John was there with his father. The trouble with the church had not been resolved, and Gerard died excommunicated. Brother Charles was also apparently excommunicated at that time but nevertheless managed to get his father buried in consecrated ground.

John Calvin, now freed from filial obligations to study the law, turned his attention to the Renaissance ideal of studying ancient Greek and Latin authors, humanist studies as they were called. In 1532 he published his first book, a very learned commentary on the ancient Roman Stoic philosopher Seneca's *De Clementia*, a treatise on the ethics of kindness and mercy. Here he could combine his Renaissance learning with his legal training. He showed already his ability to read a text with care and to explain its meaning with great insight. Here was critical preparation for the great commentaries on books of the Bible that he would later write.

SURPRISED CONVERT

At some time during his years of study Calvin was converted to the new understanding of Christianity originating with Martin Luther (1483–1546) and known today as the Reformation. Historians have worked hard to try to determine when he was converted but have not reached agreement among themselves.

Dates suggested by recent historians range from late 1529 to early 1534, so sometime between age twenty and twenty-four. This disagreement is further testimony to the difficulty of reconstructing with any certainty the early years of Calvin's life and how limited the sources for the story of his life are.

The most detailed reflection on his conversion from Calvin's pen comes in a few paragraphs in the preface to his commentary on the Psalms, which he wrote late in his life. In that preface Calvin reflects on the parallels he sensed between his own life and the life of David. Calvin appreciated the voice that David gave to all Christian emotions from the highest to the lowest, from triumph and exaltation to lament and sorrow. That sense of identification with David and the Psalms led Calvin to speak briefly about his own coming to faith. His words are worth reading:

> When I was as yet a very little boy, my father had destined me for the study of theology. But afterwards, when he considered that the legal profession commonly raised those who followed it to wealth, this prospect induced him suddenly to change his purpose. Thus it came to pass, that I was withdrawn from the study of philosophy, and was put to the study of law. To this pursuit I endeavoured faithfully to apply myself, in obedience to the will of my father; but God, by the sweet guidance of his providence, at length gave a different direction to my course. And first, since I was too obstinately devoted to the superstitions of Popery to be easily extricated from so profound an abyss of mire, God by a sudden conversion subdued and brought my mind to a teachable frame, which was more hardened in such matters than might have been expected from one at my early period of life. Having thus received some taste and knowledge of true godliness, I was immediately inflamed with so intense a desire to make progress therein, that although I did not altogether leave off other studies, I yet pursued them with less ardour.
>
> I was quite surprised to find that before a year had elapsed, all who had any desire after purer doctrine were continually coming to me to learn, although I myself was as yet but a mere novice and tyro [beginner]. Being of a disposition somewhat unpolished and bashful, which led me always to love the shade and retire-

ment, I then began to seek some secluded corner where I might be withdrawn from the public view; but so far from being able to accomplish the object of my desire, all my retreats were like public schools. In short, whilst my one great object was to live in seclusion without being known, God so led me about through different turnings and changes, that he never permitted me to rest in any place, until, in spite of my natural disposition, he brought me forth to public notice.[1]

Calvin's statement is brief and not very time-specific. Calvin's own remembrance stressed that the conversion was sudden or unexpected. His conversion was not, in his own memory, a series of small steps of change and intellectual development. He was long stubbornly committed to the old church and clearly resisted leaving it.

As a young man Calvin found himself surrounded by many friends and fellow students who were studying the writings of Luther and other reformers. The spiritual and intellectual power of the arguments for reform of the church attracted them. Some of them were converting to Protestantism. Others remained Roman Catholic but became quite critical of some aspects of their church's teaching and hoped to reform it from the inside. In this environment Calvin no doubt came to know a great deal about the thought of the Reformers and was probably persuaded that aspects of the Roman Catholic Church needed changing. But he seems to have resisted and rejected the need to leave the old church for some time. Then "sudden[ly]" the truth of the whole program of the Reformation gripped him, and he was converted.

What did Calvin mean in saying that he was suddenly converted? In his book on Seneca, Calvin had specified the definition of the Latin word he uses for "sudden" (*subita*): "SUBITA means not only 'sudden', but also 'unpremeditated.'"[2] When Calvin

---

[1] John Calvin, *Commentary on the Psalms*, Vol. 1 (Grand Rapids, MI: Baker, 1979), Preface, xl–xli.
[2] John Calvin, *Commentary on Seneca's De Clementia*, trans. F.L. Battles and A.M. Hugo (Leiden: E.J. Brill, 1969), 57.

says that his conversion was *subita*, he may well mean that his conversion seemed quite unexpected to him.

Exactly what led to this sudden conversion is unknown. It may have been some person, some event, some crisis, some reflection, or some combination of these factors. What seems clear from "Reply to Sadoleto" is that Calvin did experience serious troubles of conscience about his sin. These troubles must have played some role in his conversion.

Also important to Calvin's conversion was the issue of authority. Both the preface to the Psalms commentary and "Reply" show that. In both writings he stressed the great difference between the church's claims of authority and the authority of the Scriptures. This issue was a critical one, for he long held on to the idea that the church was the final authority even if the church needed to change in many areas. He seems to have come to a point where he could no longer accept the old church's claim to interpret the Bible against what he had found the Bible clearly said.

Calvin's conversion coincided with a growing militancy in the reforming movement in France. This militancy was clearly expressed in what came to be known as the Affair of the Placards (or the Affair of the Posters). One Sunday morning in early 1534 posters appeared all over France proclaiming the need for the reform of the church. One was placed just outside the bedroom of King Francis I. The king was not pleased. Many leaders of the reforming movement fled from France to avoid arrest, and Calvin was among them.

ON THE MOVE

For the next two years or so Calvin was often on the move. He was briefly in Ferrara, Italy under the protection of Duchess Renee of France. He also returned briefly to Paris to take care of some family and financial matters. But he knew that he could not safely remain in France for long. In early 1535 he settled for a time in Basle in Switzerland. He must have felt very much a displaced person there since Basle was German-speaking and Calvin spoke no German. The relatively small community of university-educated people there, of course, all spoke Latin.

In this period Calvin dedicated himself to writing, working on the first edition of his *Institutes of the Christian Religion*. By August 1535 he had finished this project, which he had planned as an introduction to the Christian faith. It was a relatively small book of six chapters. The first chapter was on the Law and the Gospel, the knowledge of sin and salvation. The second chapter was on faith, specifically justification by faith alone. The third chapter was on prayer and the importance of communication between the believer and God. The fourth and fifth chapters were on the true and false sacraments, presenting the biblical teaching on baptism and the Lord's Supper and denying the Roman Catholic teaching on these two sacraments and rejecting the other five rites that Rome taught were also sacraments (penance, confirmation, marriage, ordination, and extreme unction). The last chapter was on Christian freedom, examining how the Christian is free in matters of religion from all human invention and is bound only to the teaching of the Bible.

Calvin's book lays down most of the basic teachings of the Reformation in a remarkably clear and straightforward way. Calvin had made clear that Christ, faith, justification, the sacraments, and the Scriptures stood at the heart of his understanding of Christianity. He wrote about the Scriptures as the undoubted source of religious truth. The Bible teaches the promises on which faith rests: "The Word of God, therefore, is the object and target [*scopus*] of faith at which one ought to aim."[3] The Scriptures are to be trusted as true in all that they say: "So persuaded ought we to be of its truth that we must count its every utterance an accomplished fact."[4] The Bible directs Christians in all their living: ". . . we ought surely to seek from Scripture a rule

---

[3]John Calvin, *Institutes of the Christian Religion, 1536*, trans. F.L. Battles (Atlanta: John Knox, 1975), 58.
[4]Ibid., 59.

for thinking and speaking. To this yardstick all thoughts of the mind and all words of the mouth must be conformed."[5]

The Scriptures teach the work of Christ by which Christians are made righteous in the sight of God. "By Christ's righteousness then are we made righteous and become fulfillers of the law. This righteousness we put on as our own, and surely God accepts it as ours, reckoning us holy, pure, and innocent. Thus is fulfilled Paul's statement: 'Christ was made righteousness, sanctification, and redemption for us' [1 Cor. 1:30]. . . . But Christ's righteousness, which alone can bear the sight of God because it alone is perfect, must appear in court on our behalf, and stand surety for us in judgment [Heb. 11:6; Rom. 8:34]."[6] This righteousness of Christ is received by faith alone. Calvin states again and again what this faith is: "true faith" is "a firm conviction of mind whereby we determine with ourselves that God's truth is so certain," and "faith itself is a sure and certain possession of those things God has promised us."[7]

Calvin also writes of faith at greater length: "God offers to us and gives us in Christ our Lord all these benefits, which include free forgiveness of sins, peace and reconciliation with God, the gifts and graces of the Holy Spirit. They are ours if we embrace and receive them with sure faith, utterly trusting and, as it were, leaning upon divine goodness, not doubting that God's Word, which promises us all these things, is power and truth [Rom. 3:21–26; 5:1–11]. In short, if we partake of Christ, in him we shall possess all the heavenly treasures and gifts of the Holy Spirit, which lead us into life and salvation. Except with a true and living faith, we will never grasp this. With it, we will recognize all our good to be in him, ourselves to be nothing apart from him; we will hold as certain that in him we become God's children and heirs of the heavenly kingdom [John 1:12; Rom. 8:14–17]."[8] The theme of the certainty of faith in the gospel was so central to

---

[5]Ibid., 62.
[6]Ibid., 47.
[7]Ibid., 58.
[8]Ibid., 24.

Calvin from the beginning that already in the third sentence of the *Institutes* he wrote of "certain faith."[9]

Institutes of the Christian Religion created something of a sensation when it was published. Many Protestant leaders recognized in his work a gifted, young man with great potential as a theologian and a writer.

Calvin wrote this book not long after his conversion (one to five years), when he was only twenty-six years old. His theology already was quite mature. He had a remarkable ability to balance and synthesize the material with which he was working. His potential as a profound theologian was clear in his *Institutes*, although it would still be several years before that potential came to be realized.

As others appreciated this work, Calvin himself was devoted to it. From time to time throughout most of the rest of his life Calvin would return to the work to revise and expand it. The final Latin edition of 1559 (translated into French in 1560) is about five times the length of the original and became an introduction to the study of theology for theological students.

[9]Ibid., 20.

3

CALVIN'S FIRST MINISTRY IN GENEVA

When Calvin decided that he needed to find a permanent residence outside of France, he chose the city of Strassburg. Strassburg was an important city on the Rhine River right on the border of modern France and Germany. Today it is a French city, but in Calvin's day it was culturally more German than French. Calvin believed that it would be a secure place for him to do scholarly study and writing on behalf of the Reformation. He thought that a career in scholarship was what best suited his temperament. He was quiet and rather shy and did not want a public, visible career.

Because of military tension between France and the Holy Roman Empire (of which Strassburg was part), Calvin chose an indirect way out of France to Strassburg. He headed south out of Paris, planning to travel through Geneva and on to German-speaking Switzerland and finally to Strassburg. He planned to spend just one night in Geneva when he arrived there in June 1536.

Geneva was an interesting, French-speaking city in Switzerland. It had about thirteen thousand residents, which made it a moderate-sized city in sixteenth-century Europe. In all of Europe probably only Rome, Paris, and London would have had as many as one million inhabitants. Geneva was a city of commercial importance, being located on a lake and a river, and had a reputation for being rather fun-loving. Apparently Calvin had no special interest in the city.

The city had recently gone through a great deal of political and religious turmoil. It had technically been an independent city ruled over by a bishop but in the late Middle Ages had passed under the influence of the house of Savoy. Savoy was a principality located in what is today southeastern France and northwestern Italy. The Dukes of Savoy wanted to incorporate Geneva into their holdings. The Genevans resisted this and in the late 1520s and early 1530s managed to throw out the Duke of Savoy and the bishop who was allied to Savoy. They reestablished their independence and governed themselves as a republic dominated by the merchant leaders of the city.

The city government of Geneva was rather complex. Four syndics were the executive officers of the city (something like mayors). Legislatively the Little Council, composed of twenty to twenty-five members, functioned something like the executive committee of the Council of Two Hundred, which met only to decide the most important questions. In addition the General Assembly of all citizens with the right to vote (about fifteen hundred men) met annually to elect the syndics and council members. This government had a careful system of checks and balances.

In the midst of Geneva's political turmoil, Protestant preachers arrived in the city and began to have an impact by the early 1530s. One key leader emerged among these Protestant preachers: Guillaume (or William) Farel. He was redheaded, left-handed, and a fiery preacher. His effective preaching convinced many Genevans to support the call for a reform of the church.

In 1535 a public debate was held at which defenders of the Roman Catholic Church debated preachers supporting reform. This practice of a public debate had been used elsewhere in Switzerland, always to the advantage of the Protestants who were much better educated in the Bible than local priests were. Soon the leaders of the government declared that the city would become Protestant. As in other areas of Europe, with the adoption of Protestantism Roman Catholicism was outlawed in Geneva. Almost all Europeans believed that only one religion was true and only one should be tolerated.

The successful reform of the church in Geneva had occurred only a few months before Calvin arrived in the city. Farel recognized that he did not have the skills to consolidate the reform in Geneva and to organize the new Reformed church there. When he heard that the young John Calvin was in the city, he thought this might be just the man the church needed. He knew of Calvin's *Institutes* and admired not only its theology but also its remarkable balance and organization. So Farel went to Calvin and appealed to him to stay in Geneva and help the young church.

Calvin declined, saying that he was heading for Strassburg to study and write. Farel would not take no for an answer. Calvin wrote about his recollection of that conversation with Farel many years later in his preface to the Psalms commentary:

> Farel detained me at Geneva not so much by counsel and exhortation as by a dreadful curse which I felt to be as if God had from heaven laid his mighty hand upon me to arrest me. . . . He proceeded to utter the imprecation that God would curse my retirement and the tranquility of my studies which I sought if I should withdraw and refuse to help when the necessity was so urgent. By this imprecation I was so terror-struck that I gave up the journey I had undertaken, but sensible of my natural shyness and timidity I would not tie myself to any particular office.[1]

So Calvin agreed to stay, believing that he had heard the call of God in the threatenings of Farel.

Farel probably wanted Calvin to become a minister in the church of Geneva right away, but Calvin was unwilling to do that even though he had agreed to stay. He was not sure that he had the gifts for the ministry and so sought initially to be of help without being ordained. He was known as a "reader" (that is,

---

[1] John Calvin, Preface, *Commentary on the Psalms*, Vol. 1 (Grand Rapids, MI: Baker, 1979), xlii-xliii.

teacher) of Holy Scripture. Within a few months, however, Calvin had become a minister (the exact date and details of his ordination are unknown).

As a minister Calvin began to preach and to make pastoral visits. The work was demanding. The city would be divided into seven parishes that included some of the outlying districts of the canton of Geneva. The pastoral responsibility was very large for the six or seven ministers of the Genevan church in those days. The ministers worked well together, but the amount of work was great.

In addition to their regular pastoral labors, Farel and Calvin also set to work drafting a church order that would guide and organize the life of the church. By January 1537, just six months after Calvin entered the city, they presented their plan to the Little Council.

Several important provisions were contained in the articles of this church order. They called for the writing of a catechism to be used in the education of the young so they would be well-grounded in sound doctrine. They called for the preparation of a confession of faith that would summarize the doctrine of the church briefly and clearly and that all citizens would accept. Farel and Calvin presented a draft of the Genevan Confession to the city council in November 1536. The ministers wanted Geneva to be a city not of two or more competing religions but of one true, biblical religion. Furthermore, the ministers wanted anyone who would not embrace the confession to be banished from the city.

The ministers, including Calvin, clearly still had a medieval conception of the relation of church and state. They envisioned a society in which the Christian state and the Christian church were interconnected and strongly supported one another. They believed that the state ought to use its coercive power to promote and protect true religion. The ministers' ideal of one church enforced by the government was certainly not new, but they called for a level of knowledge and commitment on the part of the people that had not really been pursued by the medieval church.

In the Middle Ages a notorious heretic certainly could antici-
pate trouble with the church and state and perhaps suffer at the
hands of the Inquisition. But the church and state had made no
effort to ensure that each citizen had a somewhat comprehensive
knowledge of the teachings of the church and embraced them.
The medieval church was usually satisfied if people had what
was called "implicit faith." Implicit faith meant believing whatever the church taught even without knowing what that was.
But the Reformers were not content with implicit faith; they
required explicit faith, that is, faith with content understood and
accepted.

In addition to the call for doctrinal unity and understanding in the Genevan church order, the ministers also called for
discipline in the life of the church. Calvin and the other Genevan
ministers believed that it was not enough to reform the church on
paper. People needed to be reformed, and lives needed to change.
The church therefore needed the authority to discipline those who
violated the basic doctrinal or moral teachings of the church.

Calvin knew that the issue of discipline would be a difficult
one. On February 21, 1538 he wrote to Heinrich Bullinger (1504–
1575), the leading minister in Zurich, ". . . it does appear to me,
that we shall have no lasting Church unless that ancient apostolic
discipline be completely restored, which in many respects is much
needed among us. We have not yet been able to obtain, that the
faithful and holy exercise of ecclesiastical excommunication be
rescued from the oblivion into which it has fallen. . . . The gener-
ality of men are more ready to acknowledge us as preachers than
as pastors."[2] However difficult to institute, discipline was vital
to the life of the church.

The city council had no trouble with introducing doctrinal
uniformity for the city, but in the call for the church to have
the authority to discipline members, the city council began to
be uncomfortable. The primary points of disagreement were

---

[2]John Calvin, *Selected Works of John Calvin*, Vol. 4, ed. H. Beveridge and J. Bonnet (Grand
Rapids, MI: Baker, 1983), 66.

two. First, for the ministers, the right to discipline in the church ultimately meant that the church needed the right of excommunication. The council recognized that excommunication was a necessary form of discipline but believed that the ultimate disciplinary power should be in the hands of the city council, not the church. In the Reformed cities of Bern, Zurich, and Strassburg as well as in the Lutheran cities, the ultimate discipline rested in the hands of the civil government. But Calvin and the other Genevan ministers insisted that spiritual discipline should be in the hands of the church.

This disagreement actually was a new form of a debate that had gone on in western society for over a thousand years before Calvin: Who had ultimate authority in society, the church or the state, the Pope or the emperor, the head of the universal church or the head of the universal empire? Calvin was not suggesting, as many Popes had done, that the state was subservient to the church in all things. Rather he was asking that the church be in charge of the church and not subservient to the state in the church's own particular responsibilities. While the close cooperation of church and state was a medieval idea, aspects of Calvin's thought on this matter pointed in a modern direction in which no one institution of society would have authority over all other institutions.

In 1538 the Genevan city council adopted a motion forbidding the preachers from talking about politics from the pulpit and insisting that they only preach the gospel. The council sought to restrict the power of the ministers and in particular to limit their power of excommunication. The council feared that the ministers might excommunicate important people—such as members of the city council—and so undermine the social order. The council insisted that the final decision in a matter as important as excommunication must remain in the hands of the council.

A second point of contention between the council and the ministers related to certain church practices that had been adopted in the Swiss city of Bern. The city of Bern was a powerful neighbor and an important ally of Geneva; so the city council wanted the church of Geneva to conform to the practices of the Bernese church. These church practices were actually relatively minor matters—the kind of bread to be used in Communion, the use of a baptismal font, the attire of a bride for her wedding, and the celebration of Christmas, Easter, Ascension, and Pentecost in the church. The Bernese church was loose on these issues, while the Genevan ministers wanted to be strict. The Bernese church used unleavened bread, used a baptismal font, permitted brides to wear special clothes, and celebrated some medieval church holidays. The Genevan ministers wanted none of these things for their church.

Calvin made clear that he did not believe that these differences between Bern and Geneva were really important, but he did believe that it was important that such decisions be left to the church, not to the civil government. When the city council adopted the Bernese practices without consulting the ministers, they were outraged. Calvin and the other ministers believed that the church must decide such things for itself. They championed a disciplined church and disciplined Christian living. They wanted a church thoroughly reformed by the Word of God, by which Christians would decide all church matters. Fundamentally they wanted the city government to recognize that the church had the freedom and right to make these decisions. Ultimately the city council found this vision of the church too demanding and too independent.

The disagreement between the council and the ministers came to a crisis at Easter in 1538. Calvin had been in Geneva less than two years. The city council ordered that the Geneva ministers, like the Bernese, use unleavened bread for Easter Communion, and the council refused to excommunicate anyone for this Communion. The ministers rejected these actions by the council, noting again that they had not been consulted. The ministers decided that under these circumstances they would not administer Communion to anyone on Easter. The city council responded by promptly banishing Farel, Calvin, and one other minister from the city.

Calvin's first exile—from France to Geneva—came to an end with another exile—this time from Geneva. He was twenty-eight years old and apparently a pastoral failure. After less than twenty-one months he was rejected as a pastor.

4

Exiled to Strassburg

Exiled from Geneva, Calvin was still a young man with talent and promise, but his future seemed very uncertain. Exiled from France and Geneva and having failed in his first pastoral work, he decided to follow his original plan for a life of quiet scholarship in Strassburg.

Martin Bucer (1491–1551), the leading minister in Strassburg and a distinguished reformer, invited Calvin to become the pastor of the French refugee congregation in the German-speaking city of Strassburg. Calvin hesitated, uncertain that he wanted to take up pastoral work again so soon after the troubles in Geneva.

Bucer was a man to whom Calvin felt he must listen. He was a noted pastor and theologian in the first generation of the Reformation. As a young monk in 1518 he had heard Martin Luther preach and had been deeply impressed with Luther in those early days of Luther's growing fame after posting the Ninety-five Theses in 1517. Bucer had guided Strassburg into the Protestant faith with great skill and faithfulness. He was a fine scholar and had written long, insightful commentaries on various books of the Bible. He understood the importance of Strassburg as a key point of contact between the Lutherans in Germany and the Reformed in Switzerland. He believed passionately in the cause of Protestant unity and worked fervently to reconcile the Lutherans and the Reformed. As part of this effort, he had attended the meeting of Martin Luther with Ulrich Zwingli

(1484–1531) in Marburg in 1529 where they had tried to find agreement on the Lord's Supper.

Bucer saw in Calvin a future leader for reform with great talent. When Calvin hesitated, Bucer used language similar to that employed by Farel two years earlier. Bucer warned Calvin not to be a Jonah, running away from the call of the Lord. So Calvin again heard the voice of God in the thunderings of his friends and took up pastoral responsibilities in Strassburg.

His life there was demanding. In his first year he had so little income that he had to take in boarders. The congregation was considered small, with about four hundred members. He preached about four times a week and in addition to his pastoral work found time to study and write.

The city council in Strassburg allowed Calvin significant freedom to lead the life of the congregation as he saw best. Perhaps the language differences made it less of a concern for the council. Calvin wanted more frequent Communion than was practiced in the Strassburg churches and so introduced monthly Communion. He was concerned about godly preparation for Communion and required each communicant to speak to him about his or her spiritual condition before each Communion. (Later in Geneva the elders of the congregation would visit every family before each quarterly Communion.) He had a good relationship with his congregation there.

Calvin admired Bucer and the Reformed church of Strassburg greatly and learned a great deal from his experience there. Bucer had four offices in the church—pastor, doctor, elder, and deacon. Calvin later introduced those four offices to the church in Geneva when he returned. Calvin also followed the order of worship that he learned in Strassburg, although refining it somewhat. He was also impressed with the approach to education that he observed there. Strassburg can be seen as the mother of Reformed Christian education. A great educator, Johannes Sturm, worked with Bucer and the city council to establish a school system to educate citizens and to begin the education of ministers. Calvin based much of the schooling that he later introduced in Geneva on what he had learned in Strassburg.

Several incidents in Calvin's life in Strassburg reveal various aspects of his personality. One involved the arrival of Pierre Caroli in the city. Caroli had caused Calvin considerable trouble in Geneva. When Calvin had hesitated to sign the Nicene Creed as a creed of human invention, Caroli accused him of being an Arian. The charge was completely without foundation but for a time caused confusion and difficulty in Geneva. Caroli had left Geneva and had returned to the Roman Catholic Church. Now he appeared in Strassburg announcing that he was leaving the Roman Church again and wanted to be reconciled with Calvin.

Bucer urged Calvin to be reconciled, and he grudgingly agreed if Caroli had really changed. Calvin warned Bucer that Caroli was theologically unstable and dangerous, but Bucer, always the peacemaker, drew up a written statement of reconciliation. Caroli had signed it before Calvin saw it. Calvin felt that the statement did not make crystal-clear that Calvin was not now and never had been at fault in the troubles between Caroli and himself. Calvin became furious with Bucer. Calvin's temper was a problem that he wrestled with throughout his life. He knew that he had serious trouble with his anger, and although he had made progress in controlling it, he recognized it as a real fault in himself. Bucer certainly saw the full fury of Calvin's temper in this incident. Calvin stormed out of the room, and Bucer had to pursue him. Calvin apologized profusely, and Bucer forgave him.

This incident shows that Calvin was a real man with real faults. It also reveals that Calvin recognized this fault, and his friends so appreciated him that they could forgive his outbursts. Perhaps this struggle in his life influenced his writing. Modern readers find his writing sometimes too negative and critical. In fact, Calvin's language in relation to his theological enemies was similar to that used by most writers of his day. Usually Calvin's writing was remarkably balanced and fair. Perhaps his struggle with his temper made him particularly careful in his writing.

Another important event in Calvin's life occurred in Strassburg. In August 1540, at the age of thirty-one, he married Idolette de Bure. In Calvin's day it was common for scholars not to marry. In the Middle Ages almost all scholars were priests or monks, and that pattern tended to continue after the beginning of the Reformation. Many of the Reformers married more to prove their Christian freedom than out of a great romantic attachment. (Luther said he married to spite the Pope.) Calvin's friends thought he ought to marry for the sake of his health—he was always under strain from overwork. They introduced him to young women they thought appropriate, but Calvin was hard to please. He rejected one woman because she was too rich and above his station in life. He knew what he was looking for in a wife. He wrote in a letter that he would not allow beauty to blind him to a woman's faults. He wanted a woman who was modest, agreeable, unostentatious, thrifty, and patient and would care for his health. To modern readers this description may sound more like a mother or a nurse, but Calvin's approach to marriage was quite typical of the sixteenth century. Marriage was more a social and economic matter than romantic. Calvin, like most others, hoped that affection would grow later.

The information on the earlier life of Idolette de Bure is quite limited. She was a widow who had been married to an Anabaptist. Calvin had won both Idolette and her husband away from the Anabaptist movement and into the Reformed church. She and her first husband had two children, a son and a daughter. Calvin had provided pastoral care for her husband in his last illness.

Calvin had been married to Idolette less than nine years when she died. Marriage was often rather short in this period due to disease and the complications of childbirth. She was by all accounts a faithful, dutiful, and caring wife. Her health was not strong after she gave birth to Calvin's only child, a son who died a few days after his birth. They had no other children, although Idolette did have several miscarriages. Calvin's enemies would later say that God had cursed Calvin by denying him children. Calvin responded by saying that God had given him thousands of spiritual children.

After her death in 1549 Calvin wrote in a letter to a friend that she had never interfered with his work. This letter has often been cited to show that Calvin was cold and indifferent in his relationship with his wife. This claim is untrue and unfair. He meant this statement as a tribute to Idolette and when read in context shows his genuine affection. He wrote to Pierre Viret (1511–1571), "Although the death of my wife has been exceedingly painful to me, yet I subdue my grief as well as I can. . . . I have been bereaved of the best companion of my life, who, if our lot had been harsher, would have been not only the willing sharer of exile and poverty but even of death. While she lived, she was the faithful helper of my ministry. From her I never experienced the least hindrance."[1] In other letters he also expressed his affection and admiration for her. To Farel he wrote, "Intelligence of my wife's death has perhaps reached you before now. I do what I can to keep myself from being overwhelmed with grief."[2] He described her faith and peace as death drew near and continued: "I at present control my sorrow so that my duties may not be interfered with. . . . May he [the Lord Jesus] support me also under this heavy affliction, which would certainly have overcome me, had not he, who raises up the prostrate, strengthens the weak, and refreshes the weary, stretched forth his hand from heaven to me."[3] Beyond these brief but heart-felt sentiments, as in all matters of his life, he kept his personal feelings mostly to himself.

In July 1539 Calvin became a citizen of Strassburg. He clearly loved the city and anticipated remaining there. The speed with which he became a citizen there is especially noteworthy since he waited almost twenty years after his return to Geneva to become a citizen there.

---

[1]John Calvin, *Selected Works of John Calvin*, Vol. 5, ed. H. Beveridge and J. Bonnet (Grand Rapids, MI: Baker, 1983), 216.
[2]Ibid., 217.
[3]Ibid., 219.

As Bucer increasingly recognized Calvin's abilities, he began to involve him in the work of trying to unify the church, a work that was a key concern for Bucer. Calvin, like all the Reformers, was very distressed that the church had become divided. It seemed impossible to them that the church of Jesus Christ should remain fragmented. Luther's original goal was to reform and purify the church, not to divide it.

As the church seemed to be breaking into three camps—Roman Catholic, Lutheran, and Reformed—various efforts were made to heal the divisions. In the years when Calvin was in Strassburg, he was involved in a variety of colloquies or conferences held in various places to bring peace to the church.

In the years 1539–1541 Emperor Charles V, himself a devout Roman Catholic, called several meetings to discuss differences in theology. Four separate meetings were held at the behest of the emperor. Bucer sent Calvin as an observer to the first two of these meetings in 1539 and 1540.

Calvin had an opportunity to meet some of the leading figures of the German Reformation at these colloquies. Martin Luther was not there, but his right-hand man, Philipp Melanchthon (1497–1560), was. Calvin and Melanchthon became friends, admired each other, and maintained a friendly correspondence until Melanchthon's death.

Calvin, like all the Reformed, was always eager to pursue better relations with the Lutherans. He believed that the differences between the Reformed and Lutherans on the Lord's Supper were not unbridgeable and that Melanchthon could help. Calvin was even willing to overlook his own significant differences with Melanchthon on predestination in hopes of help on the Lord's Supper debate. Over the years Calvin appeared not to see that Melanchthon seemed unreliable to many strict Lutherans.

After two colloquies as an observer, Calvin was sent to the next two as an official delegate. Increasingly leaders looked to him as a spokesman for the French-speaking Reformed world. In 1541 a particularly important colloquy was held at Regensburg with great pressure exerted by the emperor to find some way of compromising on the differences between Roman Catholics and Protestants. Both Bucer and Melanchthon were inclined to compromise and to use ambiguous language to gain agreement. The chief Roman Catholic representative, Cardinal Contarini, was of a similar temperament. The three actually reached a compromise statement on justification. Calvin expressed amazement that the Roman Catholics had conceded so much to the Protestant position. He wrote to Farel, "You will be astonished, I am sure, that our opponents have yielded so much, when you read the extracted copy. . . . Our friends have thus retained also the substance of the true doctrine, so that nothing can be comprehended within it which is not to be found in our writings."[4]

Ultimately the conference broke up over differences on the Lord's Supper that no amount of ambiguity could cover. Calvin was not happy with his colleagues' actions on this point: "Philip and Bucer have drawn up ambiguous and insincere formulas concerning transubstantiation, to try whether they could satisfy the opposite party by yielding nothing. I could not agree to this device."[5] Calvin, while rejecting their tactics, never doubted their good intentions: "I can promise, however, both to yourself and to all the pious, that both are animated with the best intentions, and have no other object in view than promoting the kingdom of Christ."[6] Still Calvin expressed fundamental doubt about ultimate agreement with Rome: ". . . if we could be content with only half a Christ we might easily come to understand one another."[7]

Calvin here and throughout his life pursued Christian unity and devoted time and energy to seek to overcome differences, especially later through his writings. But he always insisted that unity must be based on truth. As Luther had said, "Let us have peace if possible, but truth in any case." Unity based on fun-

---

[4]John Calvin, *Selected Works of John Calvin*, Vol. 4, ed. H. Beveridge and J. Bonnet (Grand Rapids, MI: Baker, 1983), 260.
[5]Ibid., 263.
[6]Ibid.
[7]Ibid.

damental compromise of the truth is worse than useless; it is a betrayal of the gospel.

By 1541 Calvin's life seemed to have found stability and productivity. He was happily married and had produced several important writings. His pastoral work was appreciated, and his talents as a theologian and a representative of the Reformed faith were being widely recognized throughout Europe.

Calvin also pursued his scholarly interests vigorously while in Strassburg. He prepared the first revision of his *Institutes* there, significantly increasing its length. He, of course, also wrote his "Reply to Sadoleto." He also wrote his first biblical commentary there, his commentary on Paul's letter to the Romans.

His decision to write his first commentary on Romans was remarkable and bold. The letter to the Romans had been at the center of the theological debates of the Reformation. Earlier reformers, including Bucer and Melanchthon, had written important commentaries on the book. This decision reflected Calvin's confidence and determination to serve the church with the best of his thought.

Calvin's commentary was an amazing success. Much of his power as a commentator came from his determination to write with "lucid brevity"[8] as he said near the beginning of the letter of dedication of the Romans commentary. He wanted to be clear and brief.[9] From his first commentary he knew what he wanted to do and did it most effectively.

His commentary is about 250 pages long. It stands in remarkable contrast to Bucer's, which is five or six times longer. Bucer often took long theological digressions in his commentaries. Calvin from the beginning pursued a different approach. He decided to focus his commentaries on the biblical text and to pursue his theological reflections in his *Institutes*. He actually at

[8]John Calvin, *Commentaries on the Epistle of Paul the Apostle to the Romans*, trans. H. Beveridge (Grand Rapids, MI: Baker, 1979), xxiii.
[9]For Calvin's lucid brevity (*"perspicua brevitate"*), see *Corpus Reformatorum*, ed. G. Baum et al. (Brunsvigae, 1870), Vol. 38, letter 191, 402. For Cicero's lucid brevity (*"illustri brevitate"*), see his comments on Caesar's *Gallic Wars*, cited in *The Late Republic*, ed. E. J. Kennedy (Cambridge: Cambridge University Press, 1983), Vol. 2, Part 2, 109.

times refers his readers either to a commentary or to the *Institutes* for further information.

This division of theological writing and biblical commentary proved to be a most effective approach. Of all the sixteenth-century commentators, Calvin remains the most admired and most consulted. Luther's commentaries, by contrast, have great spiritual power and insight but are not as helpful as Calvin's as explanations of the meaning of the biblical text. Any modern commentator, no matter of what theological persuasion, recognizes the need to consult Calvin and interact with his analysis. He was a master interpreter of the biblical text as well as a master theologian.

Calvin chose Romans as the object of his first commentary because he believed it opened "the understanding of the whole of Scripture."[10] He underscored a point that he felt "can never be sufficiently appreciated"—namely, "when anyone gains a knowledge of this Epistle, he has an entrance opened to him to all the most hidden treasures of Scripture."[11]

At the beginning of the commentary, Calvin shows his remarkable ability to synthesize and summarize theology as he traces the development and themes of Romans in just seven pages. He sums up the first five chapters in just one sentence: ". . . man's only righteousness is through the mercy of God in Christ, which being offered by the Gospel is apprehended by faith."[12] He goes on to note how Paul in chapter 6 proceeds "to mention the sanctification which we obtain in Christ. It is indeed natural to our flesh, as soon as it has had some slight knowledge of grace, to indulge quietly in its own vices and lusts, as though it had become free from all danger: but Paul, on the contrary, contends here, that we cannot partake of the righteousness of Christ, except we also lay hold on sanctification."[13] He also summarizes chapter 8 brilliantly: "The eighth chapter contains abundance of consolations, in order that the consciences of the faithful, having heard of

---

[10]Ibid., xxiv.
[11]Ibid., xxix.
[12]Ibid., xxix–xxx.
[13]Ibid., xxxii–xxxiii.

the disobedience which he had before proved, or rather imperfect obedience [in chapter 7], might not be terrified or dejected."[14]

Not only did Calvin see the whole book clearly. He also was a brilliant exegete of the particular texts of the book. For a young man he wrote with great maturity and insight into the text. A sampling of his comments shows how succinctly he expresses the essential meaning of the text:

> *Christ (1:3):* "This is a remarkable passage, by which we are taught that the whole gospel is included in Christ, so that if anyone removes one step from Christ, he withdraws himself from the gospel."[15]
>
> *(3:31):* ". . . where there is a coming to Christ, there is first found in him the perfect righteousness of the law, which becomes ours by imputation, and then there is sanctification, by which our hearts are prepared to keep the law."[16]

> *Justification (3:22):* ". . . it is necessary that Christ should come to our aid; who, being alone just, can render us just by transferring to us his own righteousness. You now see how the righteousness of faith is the righteousness of Christ. When therefore we are justified, the efficient cause is the mercy of God, the meritorious is Christ, the instrumental is the word in connection with faith. Hence faith is said to justify, because it is the instrument by which we receive Christ, in whom righteousness is conveyed to us."[17]

> *Grace (4:16):* ". . . the promise then only stands firm, when it recumbs on grace. . . . Hence, also, we may easily learn, that grace is not to be taken, as some imagine, for the gift of regeneration [i.e., sanctification], but for a gratuitous favour: for as regeneration is never perfect, it can never suffice to pacify souls, nor of itself can it make the promise certain."[18]
>
> *(5:15):* ". . . for grace, properly speaking, is in God; and what is in us is the effect of grace."[19]

---

[14]Ibid., xxxiii.
[15]Ibid., 43.
[16]Ibid., 152.
[17]Ibid., 138.
[18]Ibid., 173.
[19]Ibid., 208.

Faith (4:14): "Faith then is not a naked knowledge of God or of his truth; nor is it a simple persuasion that God is, that his word is the truth; but a sure knowledge of God's mercy, which is conceived from the gospel, and brings peace of conscience with regard to God, and rest to the mind."[20]

Faith alone (3:21): "But if justification depends not either on the law, or on ourselves, why should it not be ascribed to mercy alone? and if it be from mercy only, it is then by faith alone."[21]

James (3:28): "When James says that man is not justified by faith alone, but also by works, that does not at all militate against the preceding view. The reconciling of the two views depends chiefly on the drift of the argument pursued by James. For the question with him is not how men attain righteousness before God, but how they prove to others that they are justified; for his object was to confute hypocrites, who vainly boasted that they had faith. Gross then is the sophistry, not to admit that the word, to justify, is taken in a different sense by James, from that in which it is used by Paul; for they handle different subjects. . . . We may learn from the context that James meant no more than that man is not made or proved to be just by a feigned or dead faith, and that he must prove his righteousness by his works."[22]

Calvin did not see Romans as a book of mysteries or theological complexities so difficult and arcane that the young preacher should avoid it. Rather he saw it—as indeed he saw all Scripture—as a clear revelation of the truth of God. Indeed, in Romans he found a particularly clear and specific presentation of the work of Christ, the gospel, and the character of faith in justification and sanctification.

The theme of confident certainty of faith is expanded and elaborated in Calvin's commentary on Romans. His study of Romans seems to have reinforced and given opportunity for fuller explication of his central concern. It remained prominent and important in all his later work.

---

[20]Ibid., 171.
[21]Ibid., 136.
[22]Ibid., 149.

Pastor

5

THE CALL BACK TO GENEVA

While Calvin was prospering in Strassburg, the church situation in Geneva had deteriorated. The city had become polarized into two camps. One, known as the Guillermins (followers of Guillaume Farel), were strong supporters of the vision of the church defended by Farel and Calvin. They criticized both the city council for exiling Farel and Calvin and the compliant ministers who had submitted to the demands of the city government. The other camp, who opposed Farel and Calvin, was derisively call the Artichokes.

As time passed and increasing numbers of citizens realized that stronger leadership was needed in the church, the supporters of Farel and Calvin gained more and more political power. In September 1540 the city council voted to invite Calvin back to take up his ministry in Geneva again. The invitation was easy for Calvin to refuse. He was not interested at all in going back.

The city council then turned to Farel, asking him to use his influence to convince Calvin to return. Farel, of course, had great concern for the church in Geneva that he had introduced to the Reformation. Farel's passion to convince Calvin to return is remarkable in that the city council was not inviting Farel to return. But again Farel recognized that Calvin was the man Geneva needed.

Farel wrote a letter that Calvin called "thundering," insisting that Calvin was a minister of the church in Geneva and must return to take up his responsibilities there. Farel even traveled from his church in Neuchatel, Switzerland to Strassburg to plead with Calvin face-to-face. With great reluctance Calvin accepted Farel's advice again. But he did not go eagerly or confidently. He was not sure that he would physically survive a second call to Geneva, and he believed that he would probably be ejected again if he did survive. But he would not be guilty of deserting his post and so decided to return.

The calls to Geneva and Strassburg offer interesting insights into Calvin's character. In his writings he seemed so certain and confident in his teaching and theology. But in facing the calls to service in his life he seemed uncertain and wavering. In his writings he believed he was presenting biblical truth about which he had absolute certainty. In his personal decisions he had no infallible source of knowledge. He did, however, put great trust in the wise counsel of friends. He was willing to set aside his own desires and instincts about these calls to follow sound advice. He did not seek to determine the will of God in these matters by some internal, mystical experience by himself. He rather looked for the Lord to speak to him through other faithful servants of the Word.

Calvin did not hurry to return. It took him a year to arrange his affairs, but in August 1541 he arrived in Geneva. On his first Sunday there, he mounted the pulpit in the leading church of Geneva, St. Pierre. What would Calvin say in his sermon? He simply took up his exposition of the Scripture at the place where it had been interrupted at the time of his exile. He was not a politician or a propagandist. He was a preacher of the Word.

In 1541 Calvin was a more mature and patient man than he had been in 1538. Although he was still only thirty-two, he had learned the value of waiting and determined to try to work with those who had opposed him. He had made clear to the city council before he returned that he thought the church order of the city needed to be revised. He had sent his revised church order, known as the "Draft Ecclesiastical Ordinances," to the city council and requested consideration of it. He did not make acceptance of his revisions a condition of his return.

Calvin's revisions addressed as one of his principal concerns the matter of church discipline that had been at the center of his troubles with the Genevan city council. He still believed that discipline was vital to the well-being of the church. Calvin proposed as something of a compromise that the matter of discipline would rest in the hands of the ministers and elders of the church with the understanding that in the extreme case of excommunication the city council would be consulted. Calvin and the city council reached a compromise by leaving a little ambiguity in the church order on the exact role of the city council in excommunication. Calvin was not inconsistent by agreeing to ambiguity here. He believed that compromise and ambiguity could be legitimate on issues of secondary importance in the life of the church but not in the foundational theology of the church. The result was that the church in Geneva came to possess a much greater measure of independence from state control than any other Protestant church in Europe.

Under the revised church order and Calvin's strong leadership, the church in Geneva took on the institutional forms that would ensure its strength and endurance. Ministers preached every Sunday morning and afternoon as well as preaching early every workday morning. Ministers catechized the children every Sunday at noon. On Fridays the ministers and others who wished to attend met weekly in a gathering called the Congregation to hear a sermon from a minister and discuss the preaching. They also met as the Venerable Company of Pastors to discuss and decide matters of doctrine.

Elders, with ministerial participation, met weekly as the Consistory to consider disciplinary matters in order to regulate and improve the moral life in Geneva. They dealt with a wide range of issues, from public drunkenness to adultery. The elders also visited families before every quarterly Communion.

The church also had active deacons to assist with the needs of the poor. The deacons would become very involved in helping thousands of religious refugees from France get settled in Geneva.

One of the ways in which Calvin wished to see the religious life of the church improved was through the catechizing of the young. For that purpose Calvin wrote a catechism that was published in its final form in 1545. This catechetical instruction was one of the ways in which reformation took institutional form in order to be passed from one generation to another.

Calvin's Genevan Catechism is not one of the great Reformed catechisms. It is too long both in the number of questions— 374—and in the length of many of its answers. It is also somewhat flawed in its pedagogy. Occasionally the question has the content, and the catechumen must only agree. For example, at one point the minister as catechist states, "We are not then to understand that these words simply condemn every picture and sculpture whatever. Rather we are forbidden to make images for the purpose of seeking or worshipping God in them, or, what is the same thing, worshipping them in honour of God, or of abusing them at all for superstition and idolatry." The catechumen must simply reply, "Quite right."[1] Catechumens may have liked this approach to pedagogy, but it did not succeed in making them express the truth in their answers.

Still Calvin's catechism has its strengths. Its theology is clear, and some of its answers are excellent. Several examples can illustrate this. The first involves God's sovereignty even over the wicked:

> Question: "Now what shall we say of wicked men and devils? Shall we say that they too are subject to him [God]?"
>
> Answer: "Although he does not govern them by his Spirit, yet he checks them by his power, as with a bridle, so that they are unable even to move unless he permits them to do so. Further, he even makes them ministers of his will, so that they are forced, unwilling and against their inclination, to effect what seems good to him."
>
> Question: "What benefit accrues to you from the knowledge of this?"

---

[1] John Calvin, "Catechism of the Church of Geneva, 1545," *Calvin: Theological Treatises*, trans. J.K.S. Reid (Philadelphia: Westminster, 1954), Q. 149, 109.

Answer: "Very much. For it would go ill with us, if anything were permitted wicked men and devils without the will of God; then our minds would never be tranquil, for thinking ourselves exposed to their pleasure. Only then do we safely rest when we know them to be curbed by the will of God and, as it were, held in confinement, so that they cannot do anything but by his permission, especially since God himself undertakes to be our guardian and the captain of our salvation."[2]

The second example is from a section on the work of the Spirit:

Question: "This needs a rather clearer explanation."
Answer: "I mean that the Spirit of God, while he dwells in our hearts, operates so that we feel the virtue of Christ (Rom. 5:5). For when we conceive the benefits of Christ with the mind, this happens by the illumination of the Holy Spirit; it is by his persuasion that they are sealed in our hearts. In short, he alone gives them a place in us (Eph. 1:13). He regenerates us, and makes of us new creatures (Tit. 3:5). Hence whatever gifts are offered us in Christ, we receive them by virtue of the Spirit."[3]

Through these institutional means and ministries the church began to take on the life that Calvin believed would provide for its health and growth in faith. Part of the genius of Calvin, as Farel had early recognized, was his ability to organize the church into forms that would propagate and preserve true religion.

Calvin himself plunged into intense activity as a minister in Geneva. Throughout his whole life he was very hard-working and productive. He preached eight or nine times every two weeks—twice on Sunday and each weekday morning every other week. His preaching was expository through books of the Bible. He usually preached on three to four verses of the New Testament and ten to twelve verses of the Old Testament. On Sundays he always preached from the New Testament, the only exception being a series of sermons on the Psalms on Sunday afternoons.

[2]Ibid., Q. 28–29, 94.
[3]Ibid., Q. 92, 102.

He preached from the Old Testament on weekdays. His sermons were usually about thirty minutes long. He also often preached for the ministers at the weekly Congregation on Friday evenings. Apparently he preached without notes directly from the Greek and Hebrew texts of the Bible.

For much of his time in Geneva he would lecture regularly at the Academy of Geneva as part of the education of future ministers. He also took active part in the pastoral work of the church, especially visiting the sick. When the bubonic plague, the Black Death, broke out in Geneva in 1542, Calvin wanted to visit the sick along with his ministerial colleagues. Even though people did not know about germs and hygiene, they did know that those close to the sick were more likely to become sick. To protect Calvin's health for the sake of his other work, the city council ordered him not to visit those with the plague.

In the midst of all this other work Calvin also found time for study and writing. Beginning in 1546 he produced on average more than one commentary per year on a book of the Bible. He also wrote various theological treatises and carried on a voluminous correspondence with leaders and friends all over Europe. Many of his sermons were taken down by secretaries as he preached and were then published. About fifteen hundred were published, but many others have been lost.

With all of the responsibilities it would have been no surprise if the commentaries and sermons were nearly the same. In fact they are quite different. The commentaries are brief comments on the meaning of the text, while the sermons have much less exegesis and much more application. This difference can be seen clearly by comparing a section of his commentary with his sermon on Ephesians 1:7, "In him we have redemption through his blood, the forgiveness of our trespasses." In his commentary on this text Calvin wrote:

> The apostle is still illustrating the material cause, the manner in which we are reconciled to God through Christ. By his death he

has restored us to favour with the Father; and therefore we ought always to direct our minds to the blood of Christ, as the means by which we obtain divine grace. After mentioning that through the blood of Christ, we obtain redemption, he immediately calls it the forgiveness of sins, suggesting that we are redeemed, because our sins are not imputed to us. So it follows that we receive by free grace the righteousness by which we are accepted by God, and freed from the chains of the devil and death. The close connection preserved here, between our redemption itself and the manner in which it is obtained, deserves our notice. As long as we remain exposed to the judgment of God, we are bound by miserable chains, and therefore our deliverance from guilt becomes an invaluable freedom.[4]

In the sermon he preaches at much greater length, elaborating on the themes of the blood of Christ, redemption, forgiveness, and freedom. He also applies the message to his listeners in a variety of ways, especially warning them against the errors of Rome:

> Now it remains to be seen how God receives us into his favor by means of our Lord Jesus Christ. That is what St. Paul means by adding that "in him we have redemption through his blood, that is to say, the forgiveness of our sins, according to the riches of his grace." Here we are first of all given to understand that the enmity which God bears us is not in respect of our nature, but in respect of our corruption. I say it is not in respect of nature because, since God has created us, it is certain that he cannot hate us. But since mankind is utterly corrupted and given over to all evil, God must be a mortal enemy to us and an adversary against us, until the remembrance of our sins is buried out of his sight. For we are worthy of eternal death until we are restored again, because God, being the fountain of all justice and righteousness, must detest the evil that he sees in us. Therefore, until our sins are blotted out, it is impossible for us to hope that God should either favor or love us.

---

[4]John Calvin, *Commentaries on the Epistle of Paul to the Ephesians*, trans. W. Pringle (Grand Rapids, MI: Baker, 1979), 202.

But let us notice here how St. Paul uses two words to express how we are reconciled to God. First, he sets down the ransom or redemption, which amounts to the same thing, and afterwards he sets down the forgiveness of sins. How then does it come about that God's wrath is pacified, that we are made at one with him, and that he even acknowledges us as his children? It is by the pardoning of our sins, says St. Paul. And furthermore, because pardon necessitates redemption, he yokes the two together. The truth is that in respect to us, God blotted out our sins according to his own free goodness and shows himself altogether bountiful, and does not look for any payment for it at our hands. And, in fact, what man is able to make satisfaction for the least fault that he has committed? If every one of us, therefore, should employ his whole life in making satisfaction for any one fault alone, and by that means seek to win favor at God's hand, it is certain that such a thing surpasses all our abilities. And therefore God must necessarily receive us to mercy without looking for any recompense or satisfaction at our hands.

Now the atonement, which is freely bestowed with respect to us, cost the Son of God very dearly. For he found no other payment than the shedding of his own blood, so that he made himself our guarantee both in body and soul, and answered for us before God's judgment to win absolution for us. Our Lord Jesus Christ (I say) entered into the work, both body and soul. For it would not have been enough for him to have only suffered so cruel and ignominious a death in the sight of men. It was also necessary for him to bear horrible anguish in himself as God became his judge, for he gave himself up in the place of sinners to make full satisfaction for them. And so you see why St. Paul has joined those two words together in this passage.

Therefore we have to observe, first of all, that we can obtain no grace at God's hand, nor be received by him, until our sins are wiped out and the remembrance of them completely erased. The reason for this is (as I said before) that God must hate sin wherever he sees it. So then, as long as he considers us to be sinners, he must abhor us, for there is nothing in us or in our own nature but all manner of evil and confusion. We are, then, enemies to him, and he is opposed to us, until we come to the remedy that St. Paul shows us here, which is to have our sins forgiven. We see by this that no man can be loved by God because of any worthiness in himself. For in what does the love that God has for us consist? I have already told you that he must be willing to cast his eye upon our Lord Jesus Christ and not look at us at all. But it is further declared that we are not acceptable to God until he has released us from our debts and adopted us, in spite of the fact that we are worthy of death before him. Thus you see that the knowledge of our salvation (as is said in the song of Zacharias) is that God is merciful to us and forgives us our sins which had made us his enemies.

Let us also bear in mind, however, that the full remission of our sins through God's free goodness, is not given without the ransom that was paid by our Lord Jesus Christ, not in gold or silver (as St. Peter says in his first epistle, 1:18), but it was necessary that he who was the spotless Lamb should give himself for that purpose. Therefore whenever we intend to seek God's favor and mercy, let us fasten the whole of our minds on the death and passion of our Lord Jesus Christ, that we may there find the means by which to appease God's wrath. And, furthermore, seeing that our sins are done away by such payment and satisfaction, let us understand that we cannot bring anything of our own by which to be reconciled to God.

And, in this, we see how the devil has, by his craft, cut off all hope of salvation from the world, by causing it to be believed that every man must ransom himself and make his own atonement with God. And that is the very thing which men call good works, merits, and virtues in the papacy. For what purpose are all those inventions that they have forged? Why do they go on tormenting themselves in all sorts of ways, so that a man never ceases day or night, but makes endless circuits and harangues? The object of all these performances is to pacify God. And so all the good works which are thus counted in popery are nothing else but means by which to make satisfaction for sins.

But that is simply to bring to nothing the ransom of which St Paul speaks here. For there is an inseparable bond between these two things, namely, that God puts our sins out of his remembrance and drowns them in the depths of the sea, and, also receives payment that was offered him in the person of his only Son. Therefore we cannot obtain the one without the other.

If, then, we wish to find God propitious, let us realize that we are his enemies till he has pardoned all our debts of his own free goodness, and, further, that our Lord Jesus Christ had to step in between him and us. For the sacrifice of his death serves to purchase an everlasting atonement for us, so that we must always flee to it for refuge.

It is that the whole life of our Lord Jesus Christ has become our ransom, for the obedience which he yielded in this world to God his Father was to make amends for Adam's offence and for all the iniquities for which we are in debt. But St. Paul speaks here expressly of his blood, because we are obliged to resort to his death and passion as to the sacrifice which has power to blot out our sins. And for that reason God has set forth in types under the law that men could not be reconciled to him except by that means.

Now it is true that Jesus Christ not only shed his blood in his death, but also experienced the fears and terrors which ought to have rested on us. But St. Paul here under one particular comprehends the whole, in the manner common to Holy Scripture. In short, let us learn to find all our righteousness in God's showing himself merciful towards us of his own free goodness. Let us not presume to put before him any virtue of our own to put him in our debt, but let it be sufficient for us that he receives us freely into his love without any worthiness on our part, but only because the remembrance of our sins is buried out of his sight. And again, let us understand that the same cannot be done but by the death and passion of our Lord Jesus Christ, and that is where we must wholly rest.[5]

The sermon, clearly, is not simply an expansion of his thought. It is an application of the text to the life of the people. Because they are so different, both the commentaries and the sermons of Calvin remain valuable resources for understanding his teaching.

Calvin was highly regarded as a preacher in his own day. While his sermons were clear and simple, they were also pointed and vivid. His vividness did not arise from clever stories or illus-

[5] John Calvin, *Sermons on Ephesians*, trans. Arthur Golding (Edinburgh: Banner of Truth Trust, 1975), 50–53.

trations. Rather it was expressed in his use of forceful verbs and metaphors with the aim of communicating effectively. As he said, "Seeing the office of a good and faithful shepherd is not barely to expound the Scripture, showing what it teaches, but he must indeed use earnestness there, and sharpness to give force and power to the Word of God . . ."[6]

For Calvin, preaching was at the center of the work of a pastor and required that a minister be thoroughly educated in the biblical languages of Greek and Hebrew and in theology. Preaching is the way in which God speaks to his people and therefore must be done with the greatest care and faithfulness. "When I expound the Holy Scripture, I must always make this my rule: That those who hear me may receive profit from the teaching I put forward and be edified unto salvation. If I have not that affectation, if I do not procure the edification of those who hear me, I am a sacrilege, profaning God's Word."[7]

Edification is central to proper preaching: "For God will have his people edified . . . when we come together in the name of God, it is not to hear merry songs and to be fed with wind, that is vain and unprofitable curiosity, but to receive spiritual nourishment."[8]

---

[6]Ibid., 941, altered.
[7]Cited in T. H. L. Parker, *Calvin's Preaching* (Louisville: Westminster/John Knox, 1992), 11ff.
[8]John Calvin, *The Mystery of Godliness and Other Sermons* (Grand Rapids, MI: Eerdmans, 1950), 56.

THE CHURCH AND WORSHIP

One of the most important tasks that Calvin took upon himself was the reform of public worship in Geneva. He recognized that for most Christians their experience of God and their knowledge of truth came primarily from worship on Sunday. He wanted to ensure that worship took place according to the Word of God.

As pastor and preacher, Calvin frequently led public worship. He prepared service books or liturgies that his churches in Strassburg and Geneva followed. He eagerly promoted the preparation of the *Genevan Psalter*, which grew over the years to include all of the Psalms in metrical form to be sung by the congregation. All of Calvin's reforms of the practice of worship reflected his careful study of the theology of worship.

As he worked on the reform of worship, several important influences played a role in the formation of his thought. The Bible was, of course, the most important. Calvin always sought to test his ideas against the standard of the Bible. But Calvin was no rugged individualist. He sought the wisdom and insight of other Christians into the Bible's teaching on worship. He carefully studied the ancient fathers of the church to know their practice. Calvin's genuine concern to follow the wisdom of the fathers can be seen in his title for the Genevan service book, *The Form of Prayers and Manner of Ministering the Sacraments according to the Use of the Ancient Church*. Also in his "Preface" to the

Genevan Psalter (1545), Calvin acknowledged especially the influence of Augustine and Chrysostom.

Of Calvin's contemporaries, clearly the most influential on worship was Martin Bucer of Strassburg. After Calvin's years in Strassburg, he closely followed Bucer's approach to the liturgy. Calvin's Sunday morning liturgy in Geneva was very similar to Bucer's.

THE PRACTICE OF WORSHIP

Calvin was concerned about the environment of worship. He "purified" the cathedral church of Geneva, St. Pierre's, where he preached. All religious symbols including crosses were removed from the interior of the church. The exterior cross on the top of St. Pierre's was not removed, but when it was destroyed by lightning, it was not replaced.

While Calvin followed that basic shape of ancient orders of worship, he was determined to remove ceremonies of human invention and to achieve a biblical simplicity. He gives a brief description of his vision of the worship service in his discussion of the Lord's Supper:

> . . . the Lord's supper might be most properly administered, if it were set before the Church very frequently, and at least once in every week in the following way: The service should begin with public prayer; then a sermon should be delivered; then, the bread and wine being placed on the table, the minister should recite the institution of the Supper and should declare the promises which are given to us in it. At the same time, he should excommunicate all those who are excluded from it by the Lord's prohibition. After this, prayer should be offered, that the Lord, with the same kindness with which he has given us this sacred food, would also teach and enable us to receive it with faith and thankfulness of heart, and that he would in his mercy make us worthy of such a feast, since we are not worthy of it in ourselves. Then either some psalms should be sung, or a portion of Scripture should be read. Then believers, in an appropriate order, should partake of the sacred banquet, as the ministers break the bread and distribute it

and give the cup to the people. After the conclusion of the Supper, an exhortation should be given to sincere faith and a confession of faith, and to love and behavior worthy of Christians. Finally, thanksgiving should be given, and praises sung to God; and to close the whole, the Church should be dismissed in peace.[1]

The ordinary Sunday morning service in Geneva can be summarized in a little more detail. The service followed the pattern of the ancient church in seeing public worship as having two basic parts—the service of the Word and the service of the Lord's Supper.

The basic order was as follows:

> *Liturgy of the Word*[2]
> Call to worship: Psalm 124:8
> Confession of sins
> Prayer for pardon
> Singing of a Psalm
> Prayer for illumination
> Scripture reading
> Sermon
>
> *Liturgy of the Upper Room*
> Collection of offerings
> Prayers of intercession and a long paraphrase of the Lord's Prayer
> Singing of the Apostles' Creed (while elements of the Lord's Supper are prepared)
> Words of Institution
> Instruction and Exhortation
> Communion (while a Psalm is sung or Scripture read)
> Prayer of thanksgiving
> Benediction (Numbers 6:24–26)

This pattern was the one regularly used by Calvin on Sunday

---

[1] John Calvin, *Institutes*, IV, 17, 43, altered.
[2] This listing basically follows William D. Maxwell, *An Outline of Christian Worship* (London: Oxford University Press, 1958), 114ff. For the similarities between Calvin and Bucer on the structure of the liturgy, see 87ff.

mornings except that Communion was not administered weekly. Calvin desired a weekly Communion but could never get permission from the city government to do so. On the matter of the frequency of Communion, Calvin wrote as late as 1561, "I have taken care to record publicly that our custom is defective, so that those who come after me may be able to correct it more freely and easily."[3] The Geneva city council permitted only a quarterly Communion (which was actually an increase over the annual Communion experienced by most medieval Christians).

While Calvin was quite content to use form prayers and liturgies in the Sunday morning service, he also recognized a legitimate role for freedom from specific forms in worship. Before presenting the ordinary Sunday service, Calvin's "Form of Prayers" stated: "On ordinary Meetings the Minister leads the devotions of the people in whatever words seem to him suitable, adapting his address to the time and the subject of the Discourse which he is to deliver, but the following Form is generally used on the Morning of the Lord's Day."[4]

For Calvin, the minister leads the people of God in worship. He speaks for God to the people and for the people to God: "For neither the light and heat of the sun, nor any food and drink, are so necessary to nourish and sustain the present life, as the apostolic and pastoral office is necessary to preserve the church in the world."[5] In particular the ministers speak for God as they faithfully preach his Word: ". . . it is a good proof of our obedience when we listen to his ministers, just as if he were addressing us himself."[6]

Still for Calvin the congregation does participate actively in worship. They must listen actively in faith to the preaching of the Word. They must pray with the minister, lifting their hearts and

---

[3]Cited in *The Liturgy of the Church of Scotland, Part I. Calvin's Liturgy*, ed. Stephen A. Hurlbut (Washington, DC: The St. Albans Press, 1944), 6 (from *Calvini Opera*, Vol. x, i, 213).
[4]John Calvin, "Form of Prayers," *Selected Works of John Calvin*, Vol. 2, ed. H. Beveridge and J. Bonnet (Grand Rapids, MI: Baker, 1983), 100.
[5]Calvin, *Institutes*, IV, iii, 2, altered.
[6]Ibid., IV, i, 5.

minds to God. They must join in the sung praise of God. Such activities are the reverent participation to which God calls his people.

Singing praise to God was an important part of the worship of God in Calvin's Geneva. Calvin recognized the power of music for good or ill: ". . . we find by experience that it has a sacred and almost incredible power to move hearts in one way or another. Therefore we ought to be even more diligent in regulating it in such a way that it shall be useful to us and in no way pernicious."[7] Calvin did regulate the use of music carefully.

Calvin greatly simplified the use of music in worship in comparison with the musical developments of the late medieval period. Calvin eliminated choirs and musical instruments from public worship, although this change really only affected wealthy churches. For most Christians he significantly increased the centrality of music by instituting congregational singing. Congregational singing was to be unaccompanied by musical instruments. The simplicity of singing and the unity of the congregation were best preserved, Calvin believed, by singing in unison a cappella.

Singing was a basic element of worship for Calvin because he saw it as a particularly heartfelt way to pray. He stated, "As for public prayers, there are two kinds. The ones with the word alone: the others with singing."[8] Calvin was convinced that the Psalms were the best songs for the Christian community to sing as their prayers:

> Moreover, that which St. Augustine has said is true, that no one is able to sing things worthy of God except that which he has received from him. Therefore, when we have looked thoroughly, and searched here and there, we shall not find better songs nor more fitting for the purpose, than the Psalms of David, which the Holy Spirit spoke and made through him. And moreover, when

---

[7]John Calvin, "Preface," *Genevan Psalter* (1545), 3. This and subsequent quotations are from an English translation (from the *Calvini Opera*, Vol. 6, 172ff.) by Charles Garside Jr. as part of an unpublished Bachelor's thesis at Princeton University.
[8]Ibid., 2.

we sing them, we are certain that God puts in our mouths these, as if he himself were singing in us to exalt his glory.[9]

Calvin believed that he was restoring the use of music sanctioned by the Bible and followed by the ancient church. From reading the fathers (especially Athanasius, Chrysostom, and Augustine) Calvin learned that the ancient church sang exclusively (or almost exclusively) Psalms in unison without instrumental accompaniment.[10] He believed that he was purifying the church from recent musical innovations in the western church. Musical instruments and complex hymnody were all part of the corruptions introduced by the Roman Church.

On the issue of musical instruments, Calvin was convinced that the fathers rightly saw that the New Covenant required abandoning instruments for public worship:

> To sing the praises of God upon the harp and psaltery unquestionably formed a part of the training of the law, and of the service of God under that dispensation of shadows and figures; but they are not now to be used in public thanksgiving. We are not, indeed, forbidden to use, in private, musical instruments, but they are banished out of the churches by the plain command of the Holy Spirit, when Paul, in 1 Cor. xiv. 13, lays it down as an invariable rule, that we must praise God, and pray to him only in a known tongue.[11]

Calvin saw the musical instruments of Temple worship in the Old Testament as having their own voice or tongue in worship, adding a sound independent of human voices. He believed that in the New Covenant only the understandable language of human voices should be used in worship.

Calvin linked the movement of New Testament worship

---

[9]Ibid., 4.

[10]For the accuracy of Calvin's understanding of the ancient church, see Johannes Quasten, *Music and Worship in Pagan and Christian Antiquity* (Washington, DC: National Association of Pastoral Musicians, 1983). The Eastern Orthodox churches to this day do not use musical instruments in their churches.

[11]Calvin, *Commentary on Psalms*, Vol. 3 (Grand Rapids, MI: Baker, 1979), 98. See also *Commentary on Psalms*, Vol. 1 (Grand Rapids, MI: Baker, 1979), 539.

away from instruments of the Old Testament as part of the simplicity of the New Covenant: ". . . musical instruments were among the legal ceremonies which Christ at His coming abolished; and therefore we, under the Gospel, must maintain a greater simplicity."[12] Calvin's statements show that his criticism of instruments was primarily directed against any role for musical instruments independent of accompanying congregational singing, but in practice he did eliminate instruments completely from worship.

Calvin argued that the instruments were instituted for the Jews to wean them gradually from the dissolute ways of the world: ". . . that he [God] might lead men away from those vain and corrupt pleasures to which they are excessively addicted, to a holy and profitable joy."[13] But the new maturity of the church that Jesus introduced made the "puerile instruction" given to the Jews unnecessary and detrimental to spirituality:

> But when they [believers] frequent their sacred assemblies, musical instruments in celebrating the praises of God would be no more suitable than the burning of incense, the lighting up of lamps, and the restoration of the other shadows of the law. The Papists, therefore, have foolishly borrowed this, as well as many other things, from the Jews . . . but we should always take care that no corruption creep in which might both defile the pure worship of God and involve men in superstition.[14]

Calvin's concern for proper worship extended also to the tunes to be used for the Psalms. He carefully supervised the preparation of the *Genevan Psalter* over the years to ensure the composition of appropriate music and in the providence of God was blessed with composers of extraordinary talent like Louis Bourgeois. Calvin expressed his basic position on tunes in these words: "Touching the melody, it has seemed best that it be

---

[12]John Calvin, *Commentaries on the Four Last Books of Moses*, Vol. 1 (Grand Rapids, MI: Baker, 1979), 263. See also *Commentary on Psalms*, Vol. 3, 312.
[13]Calvin, *Commentary on Psalms*, Vol. 5 (Grand Rapids, MI: Baker, 1979), 320.
[14]Calvin, *Commentary on Psalms*, Vol. 1, 539.

moderated in the manner we have adopted to carry the weight and majesty appropriate to the subject, and even to be proper for singing in the Church."[15] The music for the songs of the church must be reverent in relation to God and singable for the congregation.

Calvin's cautious attitudes toward music reflected attitudes that reached back through the fathers to Plato. Calvin referred to Plato's attitude toward music quite favorably both in the "Preface" to the *Genevan Psalter* and elsewhere: ". . . we all know by experience what power music has in exciting men's feelings, so that Plato affirms, and not without good reason, that music has very much effect in influencing, in one way or another, the manners of a state."[16] He believed that Plato and the fathers gave voice to the implications of biblical teaching. The power inherent in music meant that it had to be handled carefully:

> And in truth we know by experience that singing has great force and vigour to move and inflame the hearts of men to invoke and praise God with a more vehement and ardent zeal. Care must always be taken that the song be neither light nor frivolous; but that it have weight and majesty (as St. Augustine says), and also, there is a great difference between music which one makes to entertain men at table and in their houses, and the Psalms which are sung in the Church in the presence of God and his angels.[17]

Indeed the tunes of the *Genevan Psalter* show a remarkable range of emotion, carefully reflecting the emotions of the Psalms for which they were composed.[18]

---

[15]Calvin, "Preface," *Genevan Psalter*, 4. See a detailed look at this and related matters in Charles Garside Jr., *The Origins of Calvin's Theology of Music: 1536–1543* (Philadelphia: The American Philosophical Society, 1979).

[16]John Calvin, *Commentary on the Epistles of Paul to the Corinthians*, trans. J. Pringle (Grand Rapids, MI: Baker, 1979), on 1 Corinthians 14:9, 440.

[17]John Calvin, "Preface," *Genevan Psalter*, 3.

[18]The tunes of the *Genevan Psalter* with English versifications of the Psalms are available in *Book of Praise*, *AngloGenevan Psalter* (Winnipeg, Manitoba, Canada: Premier Printing, Ltd., 1987). For a good discussion of the development of the *Genevan Psalter*, see Pierre Pidoux, "The History of the Origin of the Genevan Psalter," *Reformed Music Journal*, I (1989), 4–6, 32–35, 64–68.

THE THEOLOGY OF WORSHIP

Calvin's care in directing the practice of worship reflected his sense of the importance of worship and his careful study of the subject. In 1543 he wrote a treatise entitled "On the Necessity of Reforming the Church." The work was written as an explanation and defense of the Reformation to be presented to Emperor Charles V. Near the beginning Calvin wrote:

> If it be inquired, then, by what things chiefly the Christian religion has a standing existence amongst us, and maintains its truth, it will be found that the following two not only occupy the principal place, but comprehend under them all the other parts, and consequently the whole substance of Christianity, viz., a knowledge, *first*, of the mode in which God is duly worshipped; and, *secondly*, of the source from which salvation is to be obtained.[19]

Remarkably Calvin put proper worship ahead of the doctrine of salvation in his list of the two most important elements of biblical Christianity.

Calvin often reiterated his conviction about the foundational significance of worship for Christians. In the *Institutes* Calvin noted that the first four commandments of the Ten Commandments relate to worship. He concluded: "Surely the first foundation of righteousness is the worship of God."[20] In his "Reply to Sadoleto," Calvin noted that ". . . there is nothing more perilous to our salvation than a preposterous and perverse worship of God."[21]

Why is worship so significant? For Calvin, worship was the key meeting place of God and his people: ". . . let us know and be fully persuaded, that wherever the faithful, who worship him purely and in due form, according to the appointment of his word, are assembled together to engage in the solemn acts

---

[19]John Calvin, "On the Necessity of Reforming the Church," *Selected Works of John Calvin*, Vol. 1, ed. Henry Beveridge and J. Bonnet (Grand Rapids, MI: Baker, 1983), 126.

[20]Calvin, *Institutes*, II, 8, 11.

[21]John Calvin, "Reply to Sadoleto," *Selected Works of John Calvin*, Vol. 1, ed. H. Beveridge and J. Bonnet (Grand Rapids, MI: Baker, 1983), 34.

of religious worship, he is graciously present, and presides in the midst of them."[22] The restoration of the fellowship between God and his people is the purpose of salvation, and that restoration is expressed most fully in worship. As that fellowship was broken by sin and rebellion, so its restoration must be expressed in obedience to God. "Only when we follow what God has commanded us do we truly worship Him, and render obedience to His Word."[23]

Calvin's approach to worship later came to be called the regulative principle of worship. This principle holds that the Scriptures must so regulate public worship that only what is explicitly commanded in the Bible may be an element of worship.[24] Calvin was eloquent on the theme:

> I know how difficult it is to persuade the world that God disapproves of all modes of worship not expressly sanctioned by His Word. The opposite persuasion which cleaves to them, being seated, as it were, in their very bones and marrow, is, that whatever they do has in itself a sufficient sanction, provided it exhibits some kind of zeal for the honour of God. But since God not only regards as fruitless, but also plainly abominates, whatever we undertake from zeal to His worship, if at variance with His command, what do we gain by a contrary course? The words of God are clear and distinct, "Obedience is better than sacrifice." "In vain do they worship me, teaching for doctrines the commandments of men," (1 Sam. xv. 22; Matth. xv. 9.) Every addition to His word, especially in this matter, is a lie. Mere "will worship" [Col. 2:23] . . . is vanity. This is the decision, and when once the judge has decided, it is no longer time to debate.[25]

---

[22]Calvin, *Commentary on Psalms*, Vol. 1, 122.

[23]Calvin, *Commentaries on the Epistle of Paul the Apostle to the Romans*, trans. H. Beveridge (Grand Rapids, MI: Baker, 1979), 118 (on Romans 5:19).

[24]Attempts have been made at times to argue that the regulative principle is a Puritan invention foreign to the thought of Calvin. Such a division cannot be maintained. It is true that Calvin's application of the principle was not always in harmony with some Puritan applications, but Puritans differed among themselves on the application of the principle. This crucial distinction between principle and application is missed in Ralph J. Gore Jr., "The Pursuit of Plainness: Rethinking the Puritan Regulative Principle of Worship," PhD dissertation, Westminster Theological Seminary, 1988, and therefore the relationship between Calvin and the Puritans on this point is fundamentally misunderstood.

[25]Calvin, "On the Necessity . . . ," *Selected Works*, Vol. 1, 128ff.

Calvin knew the human tendency to think that sincerity and fervor can substitute for truth and faithfulness, but he rejected any such notion absolutely.

Calvin based his great caution about worship on the fall of mankind into sin. One of the most profound effects of the Fall for Calvin was that men had become idolaters.[26] The seed of religion left in them does not lead them to the true God but to fashion gods of their own design.[27] "Experience teaches us how fertile is the field of falsehood in the human mind, and that the smallest of grains, when sown there, will grow to yield an immense harvest."[28] Even among Christians the temptation to idolatry remains strong. "The mind of man, I say, is like a work place of idolatries,"[29] and ". . . every one of us is, even from his mother's womb, a master craftsman of idols."[30]

The temptation to idolatry requires that Christians be very careful and vigilant in regulating their worship by the Scriptures. Calvin reminded Christians that ". . . too much diligence and care cannot be taken to cleanse ourselves wholly from all sorts of pollutions; for as long as any relics of superstition continue among us, they will ever entangle us."[31]

Calvin's great caution and concern on matters of worship reflected his belief that Christians too often want to please themselves in worship rather than pleasing God. "Nor can it be doubted but that, under the pretense of holy zeal, superstitious men give way to the indulgences of the flesh; and Satan baits his fictitious modes of worship with such attractions, that they are willingly and eagerly caught hold of and obstinately retained."[32]

---

[26]See the excellent discussion of Carlos M. N. Eire, *War Against the Idols: The Reformation of Worship from Erasmus to Calvin* (Cambridge: Cambridge University Press, 1986), 195–233.

[27]Ibid., 209.

[28]Ibid., 223 (citing Calvin, *Corpus Reformatorum*, 13.85).

[29]Cited by T. Brienen, *De Liturgie bij Johannes Calvijn* (Kampen: De Groot Goudriaan, 1987), 145 (from a sermon by Calvin on Deuteronomy 11).

[30]Eire, *War Against the Idols*, 208 (citing Calvin's *Commentary on the Acts of the Apostles*, *Corpus Reformatorum*, 48.562).

[31]John Calvin, *Commentaries on the Twelve Minor Prophets*, Vol. 1 (Grand Rapids, MI: Baker, 1984), 108 (on Hosea 2:17).

[32]Calvin, *Commentaries on the Four Last Books of Moses*, Vol. 3, 346.

Calvin sharply warned of the great difference between the attitudes of God and man toward worship: "This single consideration, when the inquiry relates to the worship of God, ought to be sufficient for restraining the insolence of our mind, that God is so far from being like us, that those things which please us most are for him loathsome and nauseating."[33]

He related this warning particularly to the human tendency to want worship that is pleasing to the senses when he wrote: "And undoubtedly this is the origin of all superstitions, that men are delighted with their own inventions, and choose to be wise in their own eyes rather than restrain their senses in obedience to God."[34] His conclusion on various activities and ceremonies in worship is striking: ". . . all services of human invention are condemned in the church, and ought to arouse the suspicion of believers in proportion to the pleasure they give to the minds of men."[35] These matters are so serious for Calvin because "nothing is more abominable in the sight of God than pretended worship, which proceeds from human contrivance."[36]

For Calvin, worship was not a means to an end. Worship was not a means to evangelize or entertain or even educate. Worship was an end in itself. Worship was not to be arranged by pragmatic considerations but was rather to be determined by theological principles derived from the Scriptures. The most basic realities of the Christian life were involved. In worship God meets with his people to bless them.

Calvin nowhere neatly listed the basic principles of his theology of worship. But a study of Calvin's writings and work points to several foundational theological principles.

The first principle is, of course, *the centrality of the Word of God*. The Word not only directs worship but is also very largely the content of worship. The Word is read and preached, and the

---

[33]Eire, *War Against the Idols*, 208 (citing Calvin's *Commentary on the Gospel of John, Corpus Reformatorum*, 47.90).
[34]John Calvin, *Commentary on the Book of the Prophet Isaiah*, Vol. 4 (Grand Rapids, MI: Baker, 1979), 381.
[35]Calvin, *Institutes*, IV, x, 11, altered.
[36]Calvin, *Commentary on the Book of the Prophet Isaiah*, Vol. 4, 385.

Word is also sung and seen (in Communion). The worshipper meets God through the Word.

For Calvin the teaching of the New Testament is full and complete as a guide and warrant for the simple worship of the children of God in the Spirit. No more freedom is given in the New Testament to invent forms of worship than was given in the Old.

Calvin certainly recognized that incidental matters of worship are not specified in the Bible. In such areas the church has freedom under the general guidelines of the Word to reach specific decisions that will be edifying for the church.[37] For example, the Bible does not specify when on Sunday the church should gather for worship. But some time must be chosen, and that choice should be based on what will best facilitate gathering for worship. Such decisions can be changed when necessary and can never be viewed as binding the conscience as if they are necessary for salvation.

A second basic principle for Calvin was *simplicity*. The maturity of the children of God in the New Covenant meant that Christians were not dependent on the childish props of the Old Covenant. In Christ the Christian is already seated with him in the heavenlies, and the need of visible supports for faith is greatly diminished:

> What shall I say of the ceremonies, which have half buried Christ, and caused us to return to Jewish types? "Christ our Lord," says Augustine, "has connected the fellowship of the new people together with sacraments, very few in number, most excellent in meaning, and very easy to observe." The immense distance of this simplicity from the multitude and variety of rites in which we see the church involved, can hardly be stated strongly enough.[38]

Simplicity did not mean the absence of liturgical structure. Calvin's service with its movement from confession to praise to

---

[37]Calvin makes this point clearly in *Institutes*, IV, x, 27, 30.
[38]Ibid., IV, x, 14, altered.

preaching to intercessions to Communion shows that. Simplicity meant the removal of physical symbolism and ceremonies that were not instituted in the Bible. Simplicity is closely linked to spirituality. In the simplicity of the Spirit's power, Christ is present among his people in the preaching and sacrament. Nothing may be added to that divine arrangement.

Simplicity rather than showmanship serves the pure worship of the church: "For Paul is urging the Corinthians to value or strive after, above all, those gifts which are the most effective for upbuilding. For the fault of caring more for ostentation rather than beneficial things was rife among them."[39] The eye of faith rather than the eye of the flesh is to be active in worship for the church to be edified in Christ.

Closely related to simplicity is a third basic principle: worship is *spiritual ascent*. For Calvin, Christians ascend into heaven by faith while worshipping. Worship draws the Christian into heaven in communion with the ascended Christ. This ascent in worship is mysterious, even for Calvin, but it is a foundational current in his thought. Calvin uses the idea of the believer's ascent into heaven in his theology of the Lord's Supper. He teaches that the believer communes with the body and blood of the ascended Lord in heaven and acknowledges that this communion in heaven is a mystery.

The idea of ascent is part of the pattern of Christian experience flowing from Christ's saving work. Christ descended in his incarnation to lift us to heaven.

> Now that the Mosaic ceremonies are abolished we worship at the footstool of God, when we yield a reverential submission to his word, and rise from the sacraments to a true spiritual service of him. Knowing that God has not descended from heaven directly or in his absolute character, but that his feet are withdrawn from us, being placed on a footstool, we should be careful to rise to him by the intermediate steps. Christ is he not only on

---

[39] John Calvin, *Commentary on First Corinthians* (Grand Rapids, MI: Eerdmans, 1973), 272 (on 1 Cor. 12:31).

whom the feet of God rest, but in whom the whole fullness of God's essence and glory resides, and in him therefore, we should seek the Father. With this view he descended, that we might rise heavenward.[40]

Christ continues to help us heavenward as his Spirit descends to empower the Word and sacraments of the church. "It is thus that the Holy Spirit condescends for our profit, and in accommodation to our infirmity, raising our thought to heavenly and divine things by these worldly elements."[41] The worshipper needs these means or "ladders" that God provides to help with that ascent.[42]

A visually elaborate context would interfere with our spiritual ascent, binding our minds too much to earth. "Such is the weakness of our minds that we rise with difficulty to the contemplation of his glory in the heavens."[43] False worship, especially idolatrous worship, panders to human weakness and tries to force God to descend to earth when his will is for the Christian to ascend to heaven.

> The reason why God holds images so much in abhorrence appears very plainly from this, that he cannot endure that the worship due to himself should be taken from him and given to them . . . when men attempt to attach God to their inventions, and to make him, as it were, descend from heaven, then a pure fiction is substituted in his place. . . . Averse to seek God in a spiritual manner, they therefore pull him down from his throne, and place him under inanimate things.[44]

Christians are called to worship the heavenly God in heaven, God's true temple.

A fourth basic principle for Calvin was *reverence*. Reverence is indeed a basic element of Christianity for him.

---

[40]Calvin, *Commentary on Psalms*, Vol. 5, 150.
[41]Ibid.
[42]Ibid., Vol. 2, 129ff.
[43]Ibid., Vol. 4, 52.
[44]Ibid., 350ff.

See, then, the nature of pure and genuine religion. It consists in
faith, united with a serious fear of God, which includes a willing
reverence and leads to legitimate worship as enjoined in the law.
And this ought to be carefully noted, because men in general
render formal worship to God, but very few truly reverence him;
while great ostentation in ceremonies is universally shown, sincerity of heart is rarely to be found.[45]

The worship of God in particular must express a decorum
and dignity appropriate to the meeting of God with his children:
". . . we are adopted as his children, in order that we may revere
him as our Father."[46]

As a fruit of reverence Calvin believed that a full range of
emotion, including joy, should be expressed in Christian life and
worship.

For the principle which the Stoics assume, that all the passions
are perturbations and like diseases, is false, and has its origin in
ignorance; for either to grieve, or to fear, or to rejoice, or to hope,
is by no means repugnant to reason, nor does it interfere with
tranquillity and moderation of mind; it is only excess or intem-
perance which corrupts what would else be pure. And surely
grief, anger, desire, hope, fear, are affections of our unfallen
(*integrae*) nature, implanted in us by God, and such as we may
not find fault with, without insulting God himself.[47]

But Calvin did insist that emotion must be moderate. Self-
control is a key fruit of the Holy Spirit.

Moderation is proper even in expressing joy. The psalmist
declares, "Worship the LORD with reverence and rejoice with
trembling" (Psalm 2:11, NASB). About this text Calvin wrote:

To prevent them from supposing that the service to which he calls
them is grievous, he teaches them by the word *rejoice* how pleasant and desirable it is, since it furnishes matter of true gladness.

---

[45]Calvin, *Institutes*, I, ii, 2, altered.
[46]Ibid., III, xvii, 6, altered.
[47]Calvin, *Commentaries on the Four Last Books of Moses*, Vol. 3, 346 (on Exodus
32:19).

But lest they should, according to their usual way, wax wanton, and, intoxicated with vain pleasures, imagine themselves happy while they are enemies to God, he exhorts them farther by the words *with fear* to an humble and dutiful submission. There is a great difference between the pleasant and cheerful state of a peaceful conscience, which the faithful enjoy in having the favour of God, whom they fear, and the unbridled insolence to which the wicked are carried, by contempt and forgetfulness of God. The language of the prophet, therefore, implies, that so long as the proud profligately rejoice in the gratification of the lusts of the flesh, they sport with their own destruction, while, on the contrary, the only true and salutary joy is that which arises from resting in the fear and reverence of God.[48]

He made a similar comment on the biblical text, ". . . let us be grateful . . . and thus let us offer to God acceptable worship, with reverence and awe" (Heb. 12:28): ". . . although readiness and joy are demanded in our service, at the same time no worship is pleasing to Him that is not allied to humility and due reverence."[49]

For Calvin, true worship must wed inward sincerity to outward faithfulness to God's Word. Worship must be outwardly obedient to God's inspired direction and also flow from the heart: ". . . it is not sufficient to utter the praises of God with our tongues, if they do not proceed from the heart."[50] In true worship the believer exercises faith and repentance as he meets with God according to his Word and grows in grace.[51]

---

[48]Calvin, *Commentary on Psalms*, Vol. 1, 23ff.

[49]John Calvin, *Calvin's Commentaries. The Epistle of Paul the Apostle to the Hebrews*, trans. W. B. Johnston (Grand Rapids, MI: Eerdmans, 1963), 203.

[50]Calvin, *Commentary on the Psalms*, Vol. 1, 126. Later in the same volume, 380, Calvin wrote: "It were, indeed, an object much to be desired, that men of all conditions in the world would, with one accord, join in holy melody to the Lord. But as the chief and most essential part of this harmony proceeds from a sincere and pure affection of heart, none will ever, in a right manner, celebrate the glory of God except the man who worships him under the influence of holy fear."

[51]Calvin, "On the Necessity . . . ," *Selected Works*, Vol. 1, 153ff.: "It is easy to use the words faith and repentance, but the things are most difficult to perform. He, therefore, who makes the worship of God consist in these, by no means loosens the reins of discipline, but compels men to the course which they are most afraid to take."

Calvin's labor to relate the inward and outward dimensions of worship properly flowed out of his theology as a whole. Reformed Christianity for him was an integrated whole. His doctrine of sin made him deeply suspicious of human instincts and human desires in the matter of worship. His doctrine of grace led him to expect God to be sovereign in directing worship. He would have insisted that those who think that they can preserve Reformed systematic theology while abandoning a Reformed theology of worship are wrong. Rather he would suggest that where theology stresses the sovereign power and work of God, where the priority of his action and the regulative authority of his Word are recognized, there a form of worship very like his own will emerge. A great part of the appeal of Reformed Christianity in the sixteenth century was precisely the conviction of Calvin's followers that they were worshipping God purely according to his Word. For centuries after the time of Calvin, Reformed churches throughout the world basically continued to follow Calvin's theology and practice of worship.

THE CHURCH AND THE SACRAMENTS

For Calvin, the doctrine and proper use of the sacraments was one of the most important issues of the Reformation. He devoted about 15 percent of his Genevan Catechism to the sacraments, the same percentage found in the final 1559 edition of the *Institutes*. Calvin's concern about the sacraments was in part provoked by controversy, both with Rome and within the Protestant churches. But more fundamental to Calvin's concern was his conviction that the sacraments are vital to the spiritual well-being of the faithful. For Calvin the sacraments, just like the preached Word, help strengthen weak faith as visible signs and promises of God's saving will for his people by drawing the faithful closer to Christ and all his benefits.

Above all, Calvin wanted to understand faithfully the language of the Bible, and that language is at times very strong with reference to the sacraments: "Baptism . . . now saves you" (1 Pet. 3:21); "Take, eat; this is my body" (Matt. 26:26); "For my flesh is true food, and my blood is true drink" (John 6:55). Calvin did not want to attribute too much or too little to this language. As he wrote, "Then in regard to the legitimate use [of the sacraments], two faults are to be avoided. For if their dignity is too highly extolled, superstition easily creeps in; and, on the other hand, if we discourse too frigidly, or in less elevated terms of their virtue and fruit, profane contempt immediately breaks forth."[1] Calvin sought a true biblical balance on the meaning of the sacraments.

MEDIEVAL CONTEXT

Calvin believed that the medieval church had come to attribute too much to the sacraments, making of them something magical and completely at odds with biblical religion. In rejecting the sacramental practice and teaching of the medieval church, Calvin and the other reformers were attacking the heart of medieval religion.

The sacraments, particularly the sacrament of the Lord's Supper, stood at the center of the worship and life of the medieval church. The experience of Christianity for most medieval Christians was the experience of grace received from sacraments. Baptism brought grace at the beginning of life, penance removed the liabilities of sin and renewed grace throughout life, and extreme unction infused grace at the end of life. Three other sacraments brought grace to the beginning of the mature Christian life (confirmation), to the union of husband and wife (marriage), and to ordination (holy orders). At the center of the Christian life was the sacrament of the Lord's Supper. This sacrament miraculously made Christ physically present and offered him as the sacrifice for sin. Medieval Christians had to use and cooperate with the grace of the sacraments in order to become morally fit for heaven.

Always at worship the centrality of the sacrament of the Eucharist was made clear. The priests, vital to the whole sacramental life of the church, served at a holy altar, usually elevated and the visual focal point of the church. The whole architecture of the church was designed to communicate that it was a holy space, indeed a temple in which God dwelt. The altar rail that separated most worshippers from the altar area seemed to re-create the separation of the Holy Place from the Most Holy Place that

---

[1]John Calvin, "Mutual Consent in Regard to the Sacraments," *Selected Works of John Calvin*, Vol. 2, ed. H. Beveridge and J. Bonnet (Grand Rapids, MI: Baker, 1983), 223; see also *Institutes*, IV, 14, 16.

had characterized the Old Testament Temple of Israel. For many worshippers in the Middle Ages, the solemnity of the Eucharist became so great that they did not actually receive the sacrament but gathered only to view the miracle being performed.

To clarify and regularize the medieval church's teaching on the sacraments, Pope Innocent III called a great council of the church in 1215. The Fourth Lateran Council, regarded as an authoritative ecumenical council to this day by the Roman Catholic Church, made several crucial decisions about the sacraments. This council declared that Christ had instituted seven sacraments through which his grace flows to his people. (The decision about seven sacraments actually reduced the number of rites that some medieval Christians believed were sacraments.) This council also officially defined the doctrine of transubstantiation as binding dogma for every Christian, declaring that in the miracle of the altar the bread and wine were completely changed into the actual body and blood of Christ, only the outward appearance of bread and wine remaining. The council also ruled that all Christians must receive the Lord's Supper at least once a year during the Easter season to overcome the fear many felt that prevented them from coming to Communion at all.

Because of this council, the doctrine of the sacraments was the doctrine most clearly defined by the medieval church of all the issues about which there was controversy in the Reformation. The sixteenth-century debates about Scripture and tradition, about grace and free will, and about faith and works were debates that to some extent had already taken place in the Middle Ages. The medieval church had not, however, officially settled any of these debates by the decision of a council of the church. So discussion of the sacraments, especially of the Lord's Supper, became the most emotionally charged of all the issues of the Reformation. Differences on the sacraments affected not only officially defined doctrine but also the worship of all Christians. For convinced Roman Catholics, it was absolutely clear that the Protestants on the matter of the sacraments were dangerous heretics. For the Reformers, the Roman Catholic teachings of transubstantiation and eucharistic sacrifice were absolutely unacceptable. For Calvin, these teachings led to an idolatrous worship of bread and wine as if they were the body and blood of Christ and to a tragic focus on the work of sacrificing priests rather than on the once-for-all sacrifice of Christ on the cross.

Because the medieval doctrine and practice of the Lord's Supper was so clear, important, and emotional, the Reformers devoted a great deal of time to articulating a biblical alternative. But in the first generation of the Reformation the Reformers did not find agreement among themselves easy on this doctrine. Luther stressed the real presence of the body and blood of Christ in the Supper, whereas Zwingli stressed the memorial significance of the sacrament.

THE GENEVAN CATECHISM

Calvin, as a second-generation Reformer, was eager to clarify the doctrine of the sacraments against Rome and to unite Protestants. He devoted much time and energy to writing on these subjects. But his greatest interest was to help ordinary Christians understand and use the sacraments correctly. With this in mind, a good place to begin examining his distinctive view of the sacraments is with his Genevan Catechism. There he taught his views simply, briefly, and positively. To the well-informed reader the controversies of his day are just below the surface of the catechism, but the catechism on the surface is very positive in its exposition.

Calvin begins with a definition of a sacrament:

> M [Minister]: What is a sacrament?
> C [Catechist]: An outward attestation of the divine benevolence towards us, which represents spiritual grace symbolically, to seal the promises of God in our hearts, by which the truth of them is better confirmed.[2]

---

[2]John Calvin, "Genevan Catechism", *Calvin: Theological Treatises*, trans. J.K.S. Reid (Philadelphia: Westminster, 1954), Q. 311, 131.

Here Calvin stresses that a sacrament is an external sign that testifies to God's good will to his people, serving as a symbol and reminder of the spiritual grace God gives and also sealing and confirming the promises of God in the gospel. He goes on to emphasize that the sacraments as external signs have no efficacy in themselves but accomplish what they signify only when the Holy Spirit works in and through them.[3]

Next Calvin asks why Christians need the sacraments. He answers that, first, Christians are weak in themselves and are easily distracted by this world from the spiritual blessings promised in God's Word. Second, God wants to exercise all the senses of Christians in confirming his promises. Sacraments focus the mind and senses to know that the promises of the gospel are sure and reliable. Since God has provided them to help Christians in their need, it would be arrogant indeed to refuse to use what he provided.[4]

To use the sacraments correctly, the faithful must seek in them Christ and his grace alone with faith. Christians must not seek and remain with the sign alone but through the sign by faith must rise to Christ. Faith is necessary to receive the blessing of the sacraments, which in turn have been given to confirm and increase faith. "It is not at all enough that there be in us only the beginning of faith, unless it be constantly nourished and increase more and more daily. Hence the Lord instituted the sacraments for this nourishment, strengthening and furtherance."[5]

Calvin insists that the Bible teaches that Christ instituted only two sacraments. The first is baptism, which is "a kind of entry into the Church," and the second is the Lord's Supper, which is God "feeding our souls."[6]

Calvin then examines each sacrament in some detail. Baptism confirms the gospel with its promises of sins forgiven and new life. Water as the sign appropriately symbolizes both the cleansing

---

[3]Ibid., Q. 312–314, 131.
[4]Ibid., Q. 315–317, 131ff.
[5]Ibid., Q. 320, 132.
[6]Ibid., Q. 324, 133.

from sin and the beginning of a new life. Water does not effect these blessings, but in baptism, when properly used in faith, "both pardon of sins and newness of life are certainly offered to us and received by us."[7]

Faith is foundational to a right understanding of the effect of baptism. "The right use of baptism lies in faith and repentance. That is, we must first hold with a firm and hearty confidence that we, having been cleansed from all stains by the blood of Christ, are pleasing to God; then we are to feel his Spirit dwelling in us and declare this to others by our deeds, and so practice ourselves unceasingly in meditating on the mortification of the flesh and obedience to the righteousness of God."[8]

In light of his stress on the importance of faith for baptism, Calvin recognizes that the practice of infant baptism might seem to be undermined. He devotes seven questions to the matter of baptizing infants. He explains the practice positively, but the space he gives to the subject shows his concern that his people not be led astray on this point. He states his basic approach in these terms: "It is not necessary that faith and repentance always precede Baptism. They are required from those only who by age are already capable of them. It will be sufficient if infants, when they have grown up, exhibit the power of their Baptism."[9] Baptism is still valid as God's gift even if faith only comes later.

Calvin takes his main theological argument for baptizing infants from the circumcision of infants in the Old Testament. Circumcision was a sign of faith, and "promises which God had given once to the people of Israel are now promulgated through the whole world."[10] If the sign of the promise given to Old Testament children were taken away from the children of the church, the effect on New Testament Christians "would be to deprive us of a splendid consolation which the ancients enjoyed."[11] But New Testament children are not worse off than

---

[7]Ibid., Q. 329, 133.
[8]Ibid., Q. 333, 134.
[9]Ibid., Q. 334, 134.
[10]Ibid., Q. 336, 136.
[11]Ibid., Q. 338, 137.

Old Testament children. So children should be baptized "to testify that they are heirs of the blessing promised to the seed of the faithful, and that, after they are grown up, they may acknowledge the fact of their Baptism, and receive and produce its fruit."[12] Baptism is a sign of the promise of God that becomes a blessing when received by faith.

Next Calvin turns to the meaning of the Lord's Supper. God has given the Supper to make the hope of eternal life more certain. By the bread and wine "we are taught that the body of our Lord has the same virtue spiritually to nourish our souls as bread has in nourishing our bodies for the sustenance of this present life. As wine exhilarates the heart of men, refreshes their strength, and fortifies the whole body, so from the blood of our Lord the very same benefits are received by our souls."[13] God feeds his people in the sacrament to build them up in the faith.

He insists that we receive the body and blood of Christ in the Supper by faith and then explains what he means by that: "this is not done only by our believing that he died to liberate us from death and was raised to procure life for us; but also by our acknowledging that he dwells in us and that we are joined in a union of the same kind as that by which members cohere with their head; so that by the virtue of this union we are made partakers of all his benefits."[14] Christ gives himself to the faithful and causes them to grow in grace through the Supper.

The Supper does not give Christians a different Christ or different blessings from what is received in the Word but only gives them in a different way as a sign of assured promises: "The body of Christ, as it was once sacrificed for us to reconcile us to God, is now thus also given to us, that we may certainly know that reconciliation is ours."[15] By Word and sacrament Christ gives himself to his own: "Christ, as he poured out his blood once for satisfaction for sins and as the price of redemption, so now holds

---

[12]Ibid., Q. 340, 137.
[13]Ibid., Q. 340, 135ff.
[14]Ibid., Q. 345, 136.
[15]Ibid., Q. 348, 136.

it forth for us to drink, that we may feel the benefit which ought to accrue to us from it."[16]

The catechism, then, addresses various errors on the Supper without identifying which groups hold these errors. Calvin teaches that the Supper is not a sacrifice and that Christians should always receive both the bread and the wine (directed against Rome). He also examines how the bread and the body of Christ are related (directed against Rome and some of the Lutherans). The Spirit by his "miraculous and secret power"[17] unites Christians to Christ, whose body is in heaven. The body of Christ is not "enclosed" in the bread; rather, ". . . in order to enjoy the reality of the signs our minds must be raised to heaven where Christ is and whence we expect him to come as judge and redeemer."[18]

He warns that not everyone may come to the Lord's Supper. Only a true Christian may come to the Table, which means he may come "if he is endued with true faith and repentance, if he exercises sincere love to his neighbours, and if he hold his soul free of all hatred and malice."[19]

While the catechism is an excellent introduction to Calvin's thought on the sacraments, he wrote much more about them. For example, Calvin developed fuller positive statements on the Supper in his "Short Treatise on the Holy Supper of Our Lord." Also, in over two hundred and fifty pages in his *Institutes* he both states the doctrine positively and refutes false teaching about the sacraments.

PURSUIT OF PROTESTANT UNITY

Calvin not only wrote about the sacraments, but he eagerly pursued efforts to try to unify the various Protestant camps, namely, the Lutherans and Zwinglians. Calvin believed there was a common core of Protestant belief around which all Protestants should

---

[16]Ibid., Q. 349, 136ff.
[17]Ibid., Q. 355, 137.
[18]Ibid., Q. 356, 137.
[19]Ibid., Q. 360, 138.

unite. But he also believed that certain Protestant views deviated so far from biblical teaching that they could not be tolerated. He taught that there were extreme Lutherans who bound Christ too much to the bread and wine and that there were extreme Zwinglians who tended to make the Supper nothing more than a memorial meal.

Calvin believed that the differences between sensible Lutherans and Zwinglians were not great. Luther, offended especially by the Roman Catholic doctrine of eucharistic sacrifice and human work for salvation, stressed the sacrament as a gift of God and wanted to assure that Christ was truly present and available to all. Zwingli, offended especially by the Roman Catholic doctrine of transubstantiation, feared linking the bread too closely to Christ lest it encourage idolatry. Calvin shared both these concerns and believed that an agreement between them could be forged.

From the mid-1540s until 1560 Calvin wrote repeatedly to Philipp Melanchthon, who was Luther's close associate and the leader of the moderate Lutherans. He urged the ever-cautious Melanchthon publicly to declare the essential agreement of the Reformed and the Lutherans. Calvin almost certainly failed to realize how precarious Melanchthon's place was in Lutheran circles and how limited his influence really was. Calvin had even subscribed the Augsburg Confession to show his essential agreement with the Lutherans, but he could win no similar sign of agreement from them.

Calvin's commitment to a doctrine of the Lord's Supper that he believed was compatible with the Lutheran doctrine was entirely genuine. He agreed with them that in the sacrament, as in preaching, Christ was truly offered and presented to all. He expressed this in a particularly telling way: "And this is the perfection of the sacrament, which the whole world cannot violate, that the flesh and blood of Christ are as truly given to the unworthy, as to the elect and faithful people of God. But it is also true that just as rain falling on a hard rock runs off from it without penetrating into the stone, so the wicked by their hardness repel the grace of God so that it does not enter into their hearts."[20]

Still he was adamant that Christ is received only by those who have faith: "Now, in the sacred supper Christ testifies and seals our holy participation in his flesh and blood, by which he communicates his life to us, just as if he actually penetrated every part of our body. He does that not by the exhibition of an empty or ineffective sign, but by the work of his Spirit, through whom he accomplishes what he promises. And the Christ signified, he shows and offers to all who come to that spiritual banquet, though he is enjoyed as a blessing by believers alone, who receive such great goodness with true faith and gratitude of mind."[21] Faith does not create a sacrament and its promise or cause the Spirit to work. But faith, and only faith, receives the blessing of Christ through the sacrament.

ZURICH CONSENSUS

Calvin's efforts at reconciliation with Heinrich Bullinger, the leading minister in Zurich and the successor of Zwingli, led to greater success. They were able to reach an agreement in 1549 known to history as the Zurich Consensus or Agreement (the *Consensus Tigurinus*), which was printed and circulated in 1551. The Consensus is rather brief (about eight pages) but very important to the unity of the Reformed cause. Calvin wrote to Bullinger on March 12, 1551, "The publication of our agreement was the occasion of very much joy, not only to myself, but also to Farel and the rest of the brethren. . . . How seasonable will the publication be for our beloved France; exceedingly useful, too, I hope."[22]

Several articles of the Agreement clarify points that critics had claimed were weaknesses in Zwinglian theology. First, the Consensus acknowledges the central importance of the human

---

[20]John Calvin, *Institutes*, IV, 17, 33, altered.
[21]Ibid., IV, 17, 10, altered.
[22]John Calvin, *Selected Works*, Vol. 5, ed. H. Beveridge and J. Bonnet (Grand Rapids, MI: Baker, 1983), 306ff.

nature of Christ for redemption. Article 4 states: "Thus Christ, in his human nature, is to be considered as our priest, who expiated our sins by the one sacrifice of his death, put away all our transgressions by his obedience, provided a perfect righteousness for us, and now intercedes for us, that we may have access to God."[23] This article makes clear that the redemptive work of Christ is not to be sought in his divinity alone, as some accused Zwingli of tending to do, but must be sought also in his humanity.

The Agreement stresses, against the caricature of Zwinglianism, the importance of the external signs of the sacraments as institutions of the Lord for the good of his people. Article 8 says, "Now, seeing that these things which the Lord has given as testimonies and seals of his grace are true, he undoubtedly truly performs inwardly by his Spirit that which the sacraments figure to our eyes and other senses; in other words, we obtain possession of Christ as the fountain of all blessings, both in order that we may be reconciled to God by means of his death, be renewed by his Spirit to holiness of life, in short, obtain righteousness and salvation."[24] The sacraments cannot be trivialized or marginalized, as some had accused the Zwinglians of doing. When rightly used, the sacraments take Christians to Christ.

At the same time the Consensus makes clear, against some Lutheran theologians, that the sacraments have no power in themselves. Article 12 states, "Besides, if any good is conferred upon us by the sacraments, it is not owing to any proper virtue [power] in them. . . . For it is God alone who acts by his Spirit. When he uses the instrumentality of sacraments, he neither infuses his own virtue into them nor derogates in any respect from the effectual working of his Spirit, but, in adaptation to our weakness, uses them as helps."[25] Sacraments accomplish their purpose only according to the sovereign working of the Holy Spirit.

Article 16 makes explicit the Reformed conviction that the

---

[23]Calvin, "Mutual Consent," *Selected Works*, Vol. 2, 213.
[24]Ibid., 214ff.
[25]Ibid., 216.

Spirit works effectively through the sacraments only in God's elect people: "Besides, we carefully teach that God does not exert his power indiscriminately in all who receive the sacraments, but only in the elect . . . so by the secret agency of his Spirit he makes the elect receive what the sacraments offer."[26]

Still the Consensus makes clear, in the spirit of Calvin, that Christ is offered genuinely to all in the Supper. Article 18 says, "It is true indeed that Christ with his gifts is offered to all in common, and that the unbelief of man not overthrowing the truth of God, the sacraments always retain their efficacy; but all are not capable of receiving Christ and his gifts. Wherefore nothing is changed on the part of God, but in regard to man each receives according to the measure of his faith."[27] As Christ is offered to all in the preaching of the Word, so he is offered to all in the sacraments.

Again, against the Lutherans, the Consensus insists that Christ remains in heaven and does not come down to dwell in the bread. Article 21 states, "We must guard particularly against the idea of any local presence. For while the signs are present in this world, are seen by the eyes and handled by the hands, Christ, regarded as man, must be sought nowhere else than in heaven, and not otherwise than with the mind and eye of faith. Wherefore it is a perverse and impious superstition to inclose him under the elements of this world."[28] Here Calvin and Bullinger implicitly express their sense that the Lutherans do not understand the implications of Christ's ascension into heaven.

The Consensus also explains the Reformed understanding of Christ's words at the institution of the Supper. Article 22 states that the words of Christ on that occasion must be understood "figuratively," not in "the precisely literal sense." The words are technically called a "metonymy,"[29] where one meaning is expressed by associated words. So the metonymy "this is my

---

[26]Ibid., 217.
[27]Ibid.
[28]Ibid., 218ff.
[29]Ibid., 219.

body" means, "this bread as a sacrament ministers the body of Christ to us." Article 23 explains this in these terms: "When it is said that Christ, by our eating of his flesh and drinking of his blood, which are here figured, feeds our souls through faith by the agency of the Holy Spirit, we are not to understand it was as if any mingling or transfusion of substance took place, but that we draw life from the flesh once offered in sacrifice and the blood shed in expiation."[30]

Some Lutherans mocked the Reformed notion that Christ was in heaven as a naive conception of a physical heaven. The Consensus explains in Article 25, "And that no ambiguity may remain when we say that Christ is to be sought in heaven, the expression implies and is understood by us to intimate distance of place. For though philosophically speaking there is no place above the skies, yet as the body of Christ, bearing the nature and mode of a human body, is finite and contained in heaven as its place, it is necessarily as distant from us in point of space as heaven is from earth."[31] Christ has a real, physical body that has been removed from earth by his ascension into heaven.

DEFENDING THE CONSENSUS

In 1554 Calvin wrote an exposition of the articles of the Agreement to explain and defend them against the attacks of those whom Calvin called hyper-Lutherans. Calvin still sought to convince moderate Lutherans that they agreed essentially with the Reformed. He reiterated the Reformed conviction that the Lord's Supper is a real communion with Christ. "If it is on the dignity of the sacraments that their heart is set, what better fitted to display it than to call them helps and means by which we are either ingrafted into the body of Christ, or being ingrafted, are drawn closer and closer, until he makes us altogether one with himself in the heavenly life?"[32]

He also defended Luther even though he recognized that

---

[30]Ibid.
[31]Ibid., 220.
[32]Ibid., 222ff.

Luther sometimes overstated his position: "how many hyperbolical things fell from him in debate."[33] He suggested that all Protestants should unite around Augustine's statement that "'a sacrament is a kind of visible word.'"[34]

At the same time that he hoped to attract moderate Lutherans he was willing to attack sharply the dangerous implications of the theology of the hyper-Lutherans. If the body of Christ is everywhere, is it a real human body? "Some who would make the body of Christ immense deprive it of the nature of a body. . . . Who can be offended when we wish Christ to remain complete and entire in regard to both natures, and the Mediator who joins us to God not to be torn to pieces? The immensity which they imagine the flesh of Christ to possess, is a monstrous phantom, which overturns the hope of a resurrection."[35] Calvin feared that if the body of Christ was immense (that is to say, if it filled everything), then his body ceased to be a real human body at all.

In 1556 Calvin again took up the pen against the hyper-Lutheran Joachim Westphal, producing a treatise known as "Second Defense." Although disgusted with Westphal and his deliberate misrepresentation of Reformed doctrine, Calvin still hoped to show how great and genuine the agreement was between the Reformed and the Lutherans. In the introduction he wrote, "In regard to the one God and his true and legitimate worship, the corruption of human nature, free salvation, the mode of obtaining justification, the office and power of Christ, repentance and its exercises, faith which, relying on the promises of the gospel, gives us assurance of salvation, prayer to God, and other leading articles, the same doctrine is preached by both."[36] Calvin still hoped that the large areas of agreement on so many things could lead to true agreement and mutual acceptance. Those hopes were never realized because of continuing rejection by the strict Lutherans.

---

[33]Ibid., 224.
[34]Ibid., 225.
[35]Ibid., 241.
[36]John Calvin, "Second Defense of the Pious and Orthodox Faith Concerning Sacraments, in Answer to the Calumnies of Joachim Westphal," *Selected Works*, Vol. 2, 251.

THE *INSTITUTES*

Calvin presented the fullest statement of his views on the sacraments in his *Institutes* in 1559. He discusses the sacraments in Book Four, which deals with the external means that the Spirit of God uses to draw Christians into the fellowship of Christ and to keep them there. These external means or helps in Book Four are first, the church, second, the sacraments, and third, the civil government. These helps are so central and vital to Calvin's understanding of the Christian religion that this fourth book takes up a third of the *Institutes*. Calvin declares that Christians "require external aids in order to produce faith in our hearts and to increase and advance that faith" and that "God has provided such aids in compassion for our weakness."[37] Although faith is personal and internal, as Calvin shows in Book Three, the believer must have external helps to begin and sustain that faith.

After examining the nature and work of the church as the first help for Christians, Calvin then turns to the subject of the sacraments as the second help. He gives six chapters to his exposition of the sacraments. His doctrine of the sacraments is the same as he expressed in his other writings, but here is the fullest and most carefully organized statement of his views.

Still many modern readers of these chapters at times find Calvin hard to follow. He moves easily from the positive exposition of his views to the detailed analysis of opposing views of theologians no longer well-known today.[38] Nevertheless much in these chapters is both accessible and valuable. In particular his analysis of his Roman and Protestant opponents contains much that is still relevant and useful today.

His discussion of the sacraments rests on basic definitions similar to the ones he offered in the Genevan Catechism. He wrote that a sacrament is "an outward sign by which the Lord seals on our consciences the promises of his good-will towards us

---

[37]Calvin, *Institutes*, IV, 1, 1, altered.
[38]For a full discussion of Calvin's views of the sacraments as presented in the *Institutes*, see W. R. Godfrey, "Worship and Sacraments," in David Hall and Peter A. Lillback, *A Theological Guide to Calvin's Institutes* (Phillipsburg, NJ: P&R, 2008).

to support the weakness of our faith; and we on our part testify to our piety towards him, in his presence and that of the angels, as well as before men."[39] He reiterates that God alone can make a sacrament. The promise is God's, and only God can appoint a sign to ratify that promise. In the New Covenant God has established only two sacraments, baptism and the Lord's Supper. "For baptism testifies to us that we have been purged and washed; the eucharistic supper testifies that we have been redeemed. Water represents washing and blood represents satisfaction."[40]

Much of Calvin's analysis seeks to show that the Roman theology of the sacraments both undermines the centrality of Christ in Christian religion and grossly distorts the biblical idea of sacraments. Roman religion pushes the work of Christ into the background and makes priests, sacraments, and moral improvement the very heart of Christianity. Calvin labels such a misrepresentation of Christianity "diabolical." Of the Roman Mass, he writes: ". . . by teaching that the sacraments are the cause of justification, it entangles the minds of men, naturally too much tied to the earth, in gross superstition, leading them to rest in the physical object they can see rather than in God himself."[41]

BAPTISM AND CHILDREN

In his study of baptism Calvin stresses that baptism is not only a beginning for Christians but is a blessing throughout their lives. Baptism does not merely give the knowledge and certainty of God's favor for the moment of baptism but remains throughout the lives of Christians as a perpetual promise from God. In his *Institutes* he particularly develops the meaning of baptism in relation to children.

Calvin rejects the doctrine that the baptism of children removes the original sin that they inherit from Adam, a doctrine that was taught by the medieval church. Such teaching, Calvin believed, made both too much and too little of baptism. This

[39]Calvin, *Institutes*, IV, 14, 1, altered.
[40]Ibid., IV, 14, 22, altered.
[41]Ibid., IV, 14, 14, altered.

teaching promised too much in saying that the water of baptism removed the original sin of everyone baptized. But it also promised too little, reducing baptism to dealing only with original sin and having little significance for the rest of life. Instead baptism promises the believer the forgiveness of all sins for the whole of life.[42] In the lifelong and sometimes discouraging fight against sin, baptism remains a promise and encouragement to the Christian that God is at work to save and sanctify.[43]

Calvin reiterates that baptism as a sign and seal of God's promises ultimately delivers its blessings only when received in faith. He recognizes that this teaching on baptism and faith might seem to encourage the Anabaptists and their teaching that faith must precede baptism. His response to the Anabaptists is that faith does not need to precede baptism: "But they frequently fall into this error of maintaining that the thing signified should always precede the sign."[44] That was not true for circumcision, and it is not true for baptism: "For all the present efficacy which is required in the baptism of infants is to ratify and confirm the covenant made with them by the Lord."[45] Baptism for infants confirms that they are part of God's covenant people.

Calvin's own experience showed him that although he came to faith long after his baptism, his baptism remained valid as the promise and invitation of God.

> Our opponents ask us what faith we had for many years after our baptism, in order to show that our baptism was in vain, since baptism is not sanctified to us except by the word of promise received in faith. We answer that although we were blind and unbelieving for a long time and did not embrace the promise which had been given us in baptism, yet the promise itself, since it was from God, always remained steady, firm, and true. If all men were false and liars, still God continues to be true; if all men were lost, still Christ remains a Savior. We confess, there-

---

[42]Ibid., IV, 15, 10.
[43]Ibid., IV, 15, 11.
[44]Ibid., IV, 16, 21, altered.
[45]Ibid., altered.

fore, that when we totally neglected the promise offered to us in baptism, without which baptism is nothing, we received no benefit at all from baptism. . . . Yet we believe that the promise itself never expired. . . . By baptism God promises the forgiveness of sins and will certainly fulfill the promise to all believers; that promise was offered to us in baptism; let us, therefore, embrace it by faith.[46]

If the children of the Old Covenant had spiritual promises sealed to them in the sacrament of circumcision, then the children of the New Covenant must have the same.

The covenant is common, and the reason for confirming it is common. Only the mode of confirmation is different. To them it was confirmed by circumcision which for us has been replaced by baptism. Otherwise, if the testimony by which the Jews were assured of the salvation of their seed is taken away from us [particularly our children], the effect of the advent of Christ would be to render the grace of God more obscure and less attested to us than it was to the Jews. Now, this cannot be said without greatly dishonoring Christ, by whom the infinite goodness of God has been spread over the earth and shown to men more clearly and freely than ever before.[47]

Calvin reminds his Anabaptist opponents that elect children who die in infancy before they come to faith will be saved by the sovereign work of the Holy Spirit. If these children belong to God in this way, they should receive the sign of his covenant.

If any of those who are the objects of divine election, after receiving the sign of regeneration, depart this life before they have attained the years of discretion, the Lord renews them by the power of his Spirit, in a way incomprehensible to us as he alone foresees will be necessary. If they happen to live to an age at which they are capable of being instructed in the true meaning of baptism, they will be all the more encouraged to the pursuit of that renewal by the token which they received in their earliest

[46]Ibid., IV, 15, 17, altered.
[47]Ibid., IV, 16, 6, altered.

infancy so that it might be the object of their constant attention all their life.[48]

Baptism encourages children at each stage of their growth to look to the God of the covenant.

Calvin also carefully considers the Anabaptist objection that if infants can receive the sacrament of baptism, they should also receive the sacrament of the Lord's Supper.[49] It is particularly worth following Calvin's line of thought here since today some hyper-Reformed covenantalists have raised this same question and have concluded that infants in fact should receive the Supper.

Calvin sees the Supper as "solid food," which is not given to infants. He insists that according to the apostolic instruction only those may come to the Table who can discern the body and blood of Christ there (1 Cor. 11:29). He sees this as a very serious matter. "If no persons can be worthy partakers of it, except those who can truly distinguish the holiness of the body of Christ, why should we give to our tender infants poison instead of healthy food?"[50]

He goes on to reflect on the other apostolic directions: Christians are individually to examine themselves; they are to remember the work of Christ for them; they are to proclaim his death in their communing. "Not one of these things is prescribed in baptism. Between these two signs, therefore, there is a considerable difference, as we also observe between similar signs in the Old Testament. Circumcision, which is known to correspond to our baptism, was appointed for infants. The passover, which has now been replaced by the sacred supper, did not admit all guests indiscriminately, but was rightly eaten only by those old enough to be able to inquire into its meaning [Exod. 12:26]. If our opponents had a grain of sound sense, would they shut their eyes to a thing so clear and obvious?"[51] Calvin believed that the Scripture

---

[48]Ibid., IV, 16, 21, altered.
[49]Ibid., IV, 16, 30.
[50]Ibid., altered.
[51]Ibid., altered.

clearly taught that the infant children of believers should receive baptism but not the Lord's Supper.

Calvin also responds to the Roman Catholic contention that if baptism does not regenerate a child, it does not really have any value. First, he insists that it has value for parents. The baptism of children gives to their parents a firmer confidence that God cares for his posterity. It also encourages parents to teach the faith to their children: "For it is no small stimulus to our education of them in the serious fear of God, and the observance of his law, to remember that they are considered and acknowledged by God as his children as soon as they are born."[52]

Second, infant baptism does have value for the children. In it they are commended to the care of all church members, and as they grow up "it operates on them as a powerful stimulus to a serious attention of God, by whom they were accepted as his children in the solemn symbol of adoption, even before they were capable of knowing him as their Father."[53] Baptism constantly remains a visible word to them, calling them to faith.

While Calvin utterly rejects confirmation as a sacrament, he does see value to a public expression of faith when a baptized member of the church is ready to become a communicant member. Indeed, Calvin sees the origin of confirmation in the ancient practice of a public recognition that a child baptized in the church has personally embraced the faith. He believes such a public profession is good and that children should publicly express their faith at a relatively early age.

> I sincerely wish that we had retained the custom, which I have stated was practiced among the ancient Christians . . . a catechetical exercise, in which children or youth used to deliver an account of their faith in the presence of the church . . . a boy of ten years of age might present himself to make a confession of his faith; he might be questioned on all the articles, and might give suitable answers. If he were ignorant of any, or did not fully

---

[52]Ibid., IV, 16, 32, altered.
[53]Ibid., IV, 16, 9, altered.

understand them, he would be taught. Thus the church would witness his profession of the only true and pure faith, in which all the community of believers unanimously worship the one God. If this discipline were observed in the present day, it would certainly sharpen the inactivity of some parents, who carelessly neglect the instruction of their children as a thing in which they have no concern, but which, in that case, they could not omit without public disgrace.[54]

He also reflects powerfully on the blessing of infant baptism: "how delightful it is to pious minds, not only to have verbal assurances, but also proof to the eyes, of their standing so high in the favor of their heavenly Father that their children are also the objects of his care!"[55]

ROMAN ERRORS ON THE LORD'S SUPPER

In his discussion of the Lord's Supper, Calvin examines with particular insight and care three of Rome's errors on the Lord's Supper—transubstantiation, eucharistic sacrifice, and preparation for communing. First, he looks at the meaning and implications of the Roman doctrine of transubstantiation. This doctrine states that the bread and wine are miraculously transformed into the body and blood of Christ, so that the elements only appear to be bread and wine but in reality are entirely Christ's body and blood. Calvin calls this "superstition" and mocks it: ". . . as if the body of Christ were exhibited, by a local presence, to be felt by the hand, to be bruised by the teeth, and swallowed by the throat."[56]

Calvin recognizes that the doctrine of transubstantiation is one "for which they now fight with more earnestness than for all the other articles of their faith."[57] Calvin rejects their view utterly, showing that it was not taught in the ancient church.

---

[54]Ibid., IV, 19, 13, altered.
[55]Ibid., IV, 16, 32, altered.
[56]Ibid., IV, 17, 12, altered.
[57]Ibid., IV, 17, 14, altered.

He labels their novelty "magic" that destroys any analogy to baptism. Even Rome did not claim that the water of baptism was turned into the blood of Christ.[58] Rome did not understand that the Spirit united the Christian with Christ in the Lord's Supper: "For they suppose it to be impossible for them to partake of him in any other way than his descending into the bread; but they know nothing of the descent of which we have spoken by which he elevates us to himself."[59]

Calvin warns against the Roman practice of displaying in churches the consecrated elements of bread and wine to be worshipped as the body and blood of Christ. He argues that the false Roman doctrine of transubstantiation leads to this damnable idolatry: "For what is idolatry, if it be not to worship the gifts instead of the giver himself?"[60]

Second, Calvin gives a whole chapter to focusing particularly on the Roman doctrine of the Mass as a eucharistic sacrifice. The title of the chapter shows how abhorrent the idea of eucharistic sacrifice is to him: "On the Papal Mass, by which sacrilege the Supper of Christ was not only profaned, but reduced to nothing." He seems to find this error worse than the error of transubstantiation. This Roman doctrine is "the perfection of the dreadful abomination" and "that most pestilential error . . . that the mass is a sacrifice and offering to procure the forgiveness of sins."[61]

The doctrine of eucharistic sacrifice is so offensive because it destroys the finished and complete sacrifice of Christ on the cross for sinners. The Mass "offers the greatest insult to Christ, suppresses and conceals his cross, consigns his death to oblivion, deprives us of the benefit resulting from it, and invalidates and destroys the sacrament which was left as a memorial of that death."[62] The Bible stands in its entirety against man-made sacrifices that detract from the one sacrifice of Christ.

Christ needs no fellow priests as partners in the offering of

---

[58]Ibid., IV, 17, 15.
[59]Ibid., IV, 17, 16, altered.
[60]Ibid., IV, 17, 36.
[61]Ibid., IV, 18, 1, altered.
[62]Ibid.

propitiatory sacrifices,[63] and his sacrifice on the cross cannot be repeated.[64] In Calvin's day some Roman theologians such as John Eck called the Mass a repetition of Christ's sacrifice. Since that time Rome insists that the Mass is not a repetition but a continuation of the one sacrifice on the cross. Calvin had heard that argument in his day too and rejected it as vigorously as the idea that the Mass was a repetition of Christ's sacrifice.

> The more artful sophists have recourse to a deeper deception, namely that it is not a repetition of that sacrifice, but an application of it. This sophistry may also be refuted, without any more difficulty than the former. For Christ once offered himself up, not that his sacrifice might be daily ratified by new offerings, but that the benefit of it might be communicated to us by the preaching of the gospel and the administration of the sacred supper.[65]

Any language that continues to make of the Mass a propitiatory sacrifice to God destroys or denies the finished work of Christ on the cross.

Calvin is adamant that the idea of the Lord's Supper as a propitiatory sacrifice not only undermines the sacrifice of Christ but also fundamentally distorts and destroys the meaning of the sacrament. It turns the sacrament upside down, changing it from a gift that God gives to his people into an offering that the church gives to God: "For the supper itself is a gift of God, which ought to be received with thanksgiving. The sacrifice of the mass is pretended to be a price given to God and received by him as a satisfaction. As far as giving differs from receiving, so far does the sacrifice of the mass differ from the sacrament of the supper."[66]

Third, Calvin shows that the Roman errors of transubstantiation and eucharistic sacrifice also contribute to its error on worthy communing. Rome insisted that communicants had to

---

[63]Ibid., IV, 18, 2.
[64]Ibid., IV, 18, 3.
[65]Ibid., altered.
[66]Ibid., IV, 18, 7, altered.

purify their souls through the sacrament of penance before coming to the altar. The grace that the Eucharist brings to the soul must be properly prepared for. While Calvin taught that only repentant believers could come to the Supper, he saw that Rome had missed the point of the sacrament, namely, to help sinners. He knew that even those who have most pursued holiness are not worthy of coming to the Table in themselves.[67] Rather it is those who know themselves to be sinners and recognize their need of Christ who should come: ". . . let us remember that this sacred banquet is medicine to the sick, comfort to the sinner, alms to the poor."[68]

True Christians come to the Supper acknowledging their sin and their need of Christ. "Therefore, the best and only worthiness that we can present to God is to offer him our vileness and unworthiness, that he may make us worthy of his mercy; to despair in ourselves, that we may find consolation in him; to humble ourselves, that we may be exalted by him; to accuse ourselves, that we may be justified by him." Calvin called Christians to come to the Table if they have faith in Christ and see in themselves a love that is the beginning of the sanctifying work of the Holy Spirit: ". . . the worthiness which is required by God consists chiefly in faith, which attributes every thing to Christ, and places no dependence on ourselves, and, secondly, in love, even that love which it is enough for us to present to God in an imperfect state, that he may increase and improve it; for we cannot produce it in a state of perfection."[69]

CONCLUSION

Calvin throughout his life gave a great deal of attention to the sacraments because they were so important to him. God has given the Lord's Supper "to sustain and nourish us as long as we live" and to be our "pledge, as a further assurance of this never-

---

[67]Ibid., IV, 17, 41.
[68]Ibid., IV, 17, 42.
[69]Ibid., altered.

ceasing liberality."[70] Properly used and understood, the sacrament "nourishes, refreshes, strengthens, and exhilarates."[71] For Calvin the truth of the sacraments is fundamentally simple. In the sacraments, "We must hunger after Christ, we must seek, contemplate, and learn him alone."[72]

---

[70]Ibid., IV, 17, 1.
[71]Ibid., IV, 17, 3.
[72]Ibid., IV, 18, 20.

THE CHURCH AND PREDESTINATION

Today if anything is remembered about John Calvin, it is that he taught the doctrine of predestination. Those who remember this almost invariably see it as a black mark against him. For many predestination is a cold and gloomy doctrine, leading only to fear and fatalism. But for Calvin and those who followed him predestination was a vital and comforting doctrine. Calvin did write quite a bit about predestination, not because it was so central to his theology, but because this biblical truth was so often attacked in his time.

CALVIN AND CONTROVERSY

One case of such an attack was launched against Calvin and his doctrine of predestination by a French refugee who arrived in Geneva in 1550 named Jerome Bolsec. He was an excellent physician and in a short time became the personal physician to a noble French refugee with whom Calvin was very friendly. Bolsec was also a former monk and was a doctor of theology. He continued to be interested in theology and often attended the weekly Congregation meeting, which included a sermon and discussion. The meetings were primarily for ministers, but others were welcome to attend.

One evening in October 1551 when Calvin was out of town,

Farel, who was visiting the city, preached the sermon at the Congregation meeting. He preached on predestination, and after the sermon Bolsec rose to attack his views vehemently. Bolsec was clearly using the occasion to attack Calvin through Farel. But Bolsec was unaware that Calvin had returned from his trip early, had entered the meeting late, and was sitting in the back. When Bolsec finished, Calvin rose and presented a lengthy, extemporaneous defense of the doctrine of predestination. Those who heard him that night thought the defense was remarkably powerful, but Bolsec was not persuaded.

The differences between Bolsec and Calvin became a growing point of discussion in the city. Bolsec believed that Calvin's understanding of predestination was erroneous and absurd and that Calvin himself was a false interpreter of the Bible. Such a charge against a minister was a serious matter, and Bolsec was imprisoned. This was the first serious theological challenge to Calvin in Geneva since his return in 1541.

Calvin urged that other cities be consulted, and the Genevan city council wrote to Basel, Bern, Zurich, and Neuchatel for advice. The letter, which Calvin must have helped write, describes Bolsec as one "who, having thrown off the monk's cowl, is become one of those strolling physicians, who, by habitual deception and trickery, acquire a degree of impudence which makes them prompt and ready in venturing upon anything whatever."[1] The letter expresses the view of Calvin and his ministerial colleagues that the doctrine of election is "all-important"[2] as a foundation of true religion. A proper understanding of predestination is necessary for a proper understanding of faith and justification: "That we are justified by faith, we all agree; but the real mercy of God can only be perceived when we learn that faith is the fruit of free adoption, and that, in point of fact, adoption flows from the eternal election of God."[3] The council hoped that the ministers

---

[1]John Calvin, *Selected Works*, Vol. 5, ed. H. Beveridge and J. Bonnet (Grand Rapids, MI: Baker, 1983), 322ff.
[2]Ibid., 323.
[3]Ibid., 324.

from other cities would affirm this critical role for the doctrine of predestination.

The council specifically sought advice from the other cities on the errors of Bolsec who, first, claimed that election is a novel doctrine invented by Lorenzo Valla and, second, affirmed "that men are not saved because they have been elected, but that they are elected because they believe; that no one is condemned at the mere pleasure of God; that those only are condemned who deprive themselves of the election common to all."[4] Although the letter sought the response of the ministers of the other Swiss cities, the Genevan ministers made it clear that they stood by the doctrine of predestination presented in Calvin's *Institutes*. They commended the book's "reverence and sobriety" and declared that it is "its own bright witness"[5] to this truth.

Aside from Neuchatel where Farel was the preacher, the responses were disappointing. The cities were weak in their defense of the doctrine of predestination. Calvin was particularly disappointed in the response of his friend from Zurich, Heinrich Bullinger.[6] Calvin in his own day faced not only strong opposition to his doctrine of predestination but also at times only lukewarm support. Still by the end of 1551 the city council and the church in Geneva had decided against Bolsec, and he was exiled from the city.

Calvin knew that the doctrine of predestination was difficult to understand and could be dangerously misused. He once wrote, "The discussion of predestination—a subject of itself rather intricate—is made very perplexed, and therefore dangerous, by human curiosity."[7] By "curiosity" Calvin means the human desire to ask questions to which God has not revealed the answers. Calvin's approach to predestination was to ask what God had revealed in the Bible and not to inquire any further than that. He wrote, "We should neither scrutinize those things

---

[4]Ibid., 323.
[5]Ibid., 324.
[6]For a fuller discussion of the Bolsec controversy, see W. R. Godfrey, *Reformation Sketches* (Phillipsburg, NJ: P&R, 2003), 87–98.
[7]John Calvin, *Institutes*, III, 21, 1.

which the Lord has left concealed, nor neglect those which he has openly exhibited, lest we be condemned for excessive curiosity on the one hand, or for ingratitude on the other."[8] On this point Calvin often cited Deuteronomy 29:29: "The secret things belong to the LORD our God, but the things that are revealed belong to us and to our children forever, that we may do all the words of this law."

Bolsec's position on predestination was that God had decreed that all who believed would be saved. God had not determined who would believe and who would not. Faith depended on human response. Bolsec's position was one that had often been held in the church historically, but Calvin believed that it was unbiblical and shallow.

Calvin agreed that everyone who believed in Christ would be saved, but he denied that this was the whole biblical teaching on election. He insisted that the Bible also answers the question, why is it that some believe and some do not? The answer was not, as many believed, that some exercise their free will to believe while others do not. While that answer may seem fair and encourages human responsibility, Calvin believed the Bible does not teach that sinners have free will to turn to God. The idea of free will does not take the disastrous effect of sin on human nature seriously enough. Romans 3:10–11 says, "None is righteous, no, not one; no one understands; no one seeks for God." The unregenerate human will acts only to resist God.

Bolsec's views undermine the work of Christ, reducing him from being a real and complete Savior to being only a potential savior. Also he does not account for the teaching of Ephesians 1 about God's plan from before the foundation of the world.

For Calvin predestination is not simply a biblical truth but is foundational to understanding biblical religion. Bolsec's religion is man-centered: God has done all he can to save, but the ultimate decision on salvation rests with the human response. For Calvin

---

[8]Ibid., III, 21, 4.

such religion takes the glory of salvation away from God and trivializes the work of Christ.

In 1552 in Geneva problems on the doctrine of predestination for Calvin continued. A nobleman named John Trolliet, only recently having left the Roman Church, attacked Calvin on predestination, accusing him of making God the author of sin. Those charges were heard and rejected by the city council in October 1552. But part of the harm that Trolliet tried to cause was to suggest that Melanchthon also opposed Calvin on this doctrine. There were indeed significant differences between Calvin and Melanchthon, but the differences never caused a serious confrontation between them. Calvin wrote Melanchthon a letter on November 28, 1552 full of assurances of his high regard and personal affection for Melanchthon. The letter also contains a strong encouragement to Melanchthon to adopt a clear, biblical position on predestination. Calvin's arguments in this letter are a particularly brief and forceful presentation of his own views:

> But, to speak candidly, religious scruples prevent me from agreeing with you on this point of doctrine, for you appear to discuss the freedom of the will in too philosophical a manner; and in treating the doctrine of election, you seem to have no other purpose, save that you may suit yourself to the common feeling of mankind. And it cannot be attributed to hallucination, that you, a man acute and wise, and deeply versed in Scripture, confound the election of God with its promises which are universal. For nothing is more certain than that the Gospel is addressed to all promiscuously, but that the Spirit of faith is bestowed on the elect alone, by peculiar privilege. The promises are universal. How does it happen, therefore, that their efficacy is not equally felt by all? For this reason: because God does not reveal his arm to all. Indeed, among men but moderately skilled in Scripture, this subject needs not to be discussed, seeing that the promises of the Gospel make offer of the grace of Christ equally to all; and God, by the external call, invites all who are willing to accept of salvation. Faith, also, is a special gift.[9]

---

[9]Calvin, *Selected Works*, Vol. 5, 379ff.

Here Calvin lays out clearly that while God's promises are offered to all, they are received only by the elect of God as they are moved by his grace. Calvin does not seem to have convinced Melanchthon, but their friendship continued intact.

Although again he was successful in defending himself against Trolliet, he feared that the power of his opponents in the city seemed to be rising. Those fears seemed fulfilled in the elections of February 1553 as the enemies of a disciplined church were elected to office. By July 1553 tensions had risen so high that Calvin offered his resignation to the city council. After twelve years of diligent work he thought his ministry in Geneva had at last come to an end. The new leaders of the council, however, had come to realize that although they did not like Calvin, they did not know how they could get along without him. They recognized that they needed his brilliance and effectiveness. They wanted to tame him, not eliminate him, and so they rejected his resignation.

THE DOCTRINE OF PREDESTINATION FOR CALVIN

Calvin did not make the doctrine of predestination the centerpiece of his teaching by any means. He makes only a few passing references to it in his 1536 *Institutes*. No single question in his 1545 Catechism is devoted to the subject. Still he believed that the doctrine was important because it is taught in Scripture and because it underscores that salvation is entirely the work and gift of God and that man contributes nothing at all to it. To this point Calvin agrees with others in the history of the church who had taught the doctrine of predestination.

The doctrine of predestination is no novelty of Calvin. Calvin believed strongly that this doctrine was taught clearly throughout Scripture and particularly by the apostle Paul. This doctrine was also taught by the great church father Augustine and by many medieval theologians, including Thomas Aquinas. The leading reformers including Martin Luther and Ulrich Zwingli also certainly taught it.

The point at which Calvin goes beyond other theologians, recapturing a key Pauline emphasis, is to insist that predestination is a practical doctrine. Calvin taught that each Christian can and should know that he or she is elect and from that election derive comfort and assurance in the face of doubt and temptations. Calvinism alone teaches that Christians not only can know that they are saved in the present but may also be assured that they will continue to be saved in the future.

Again Calvin's critics have often accused him of speculating about predestination and constructing a rationalistic system. Calvin utterly rejected any such approach to the doctrine. "... to desire any other knowledge of predestination than what is unfolded in the word of God, indicates as great a folly as a wish to walk through unpassable roads, or to see in the dark. Nor let us be ashamed to be ignorant of some things relative to a subject in which there is a kind of learned ignorance."[10] He sought only to be biblical.

Calvin taught predestination because he found it present in the Bible, a doctrine, he concluded, both unavoidable and profitable. "For the Scripture is the school of the Holy Spirit, in which, as nothing necessary and useful to be known is omitted, so nothing is taught which is not beneficial to know."[11]

For Calvin the true rationalists are those who want to know more about this doctrine than God has revealed in his Word. The pursuit of such knowledge is indeed dangerous.

> The predestination of God is indeed in reality a labyrinth, from which the mind of man can by no means extricate itself: but so unreasonable is the curiosity of man, that the more perilous the examination of the subject, the more boldly he proceeds; so that when predestination is discussed, as he cannot restrain himself within due limits, he immediately, through his rashness, plunges himself, as it were, into the depth of the sea. What remedy is there for the godly? Must they avoid every thought of predestination? By no means: for as the Holy Spirit has taught us nothing but

---

[10]Calvin, *Institutes*, III, 21, 2, altered.
[11]Ibid., III, 21, 3.

what it behooves us to know, the knowledge of this will no doubt be useful, provided it be confined to the word of God.[12]

A SIMPLE DOCTRINE

Calvin continued to insist that predestination was a very important doctrine to teach.

> We shall never be clearly convinced as we ought to be, that our salvation flows from the fountain of God's free mercy, till we come to know his eternal election, which illustrates the grace of God by this comparison, that he adopts not all promiscuously to the hope of salvation but gives to some what he refuses to others. Ignorance of this principle evidently detracts from God's glory, and diminishes true humility.[13]

Some critics of Calvinism have argued that his doctrine of predestination and the sovereignty of God must empty human experience and action of all meaning. Calvin rejected any such notion. God works in history and through humans to accomplish his eternal purpose. God not only chooses the elect in eternity but calls and gathers them in history. "Though they indeed, whom God in his eternal counsel has destined as sons to himself, are perpetually sons, yet Scripture in many parts counts none to be God's children but those, the election of whom has been proved by their calling: and hence he teaches us not to judge, much less decide, respecting God's election, except as far as it manifests itself by its own evidences."[14]

Calvin makes clear that humans will indeed be active in the service of God, but that action is entirely the work of God's grace. "They are, however, to be condemned who remain secure and idle on the pretence of giving place to the grace of God; for though nothing is done by their own striving, yet that effort which is influenced by God is not ineffectual . . . we may hence learn to ask

---

[12]John Calvin, *Commentaries on the Epistle of Paul the Apostle to the Romans*, trans. H. Beveridge (Grand Rapids, MI: Baker, 1979), on Rom. 9:14, 353ff.
[13]Calvin, *Institutes*, III, 21, 1, altered.
[14]Calvin, *Commentaries on the Epistle of Paul the Apostle to the Romans*, on Rom. 9:26, 372ff.

all things of him, to hope for all things from him, and to ascribe all things to him, while we are prosecuting the work of our salvation with fear and trembling."[15]

God particularly uses preaching to gather his elect. "For though the preaching of the gospel is a stream from the source of election, yet because it is common also to the reprobate, it would of itself be no solid proof of election. For God effectively teaches his elect to bring them to faith."[16] Preaching becomes effective in the elect only by the work of the Holy Spirit in the hearts of the elect. "This point is further demonstrated by the very nature and dispensation of calling, which consists not only in the preaching of the Word, but also in the accompanying illumination of the Spirit. . . . This internal call, therefore, is a pledge of salvation which cannot possibly deceive us. To this purpose is that passage of John: 'And by this we know that he abides in us, by the Spirit whom he has given us.'"[17]

REPROBATION

While the predestination of the elect to life can easily be presented as a positive and comforting doctrine, the predestination of the reprobate to damnation has been especially troubling to many. Calvin did not shrink from articulating the doctrine of reprobation. As God is sovereign in saving some sinners from their lost condition, so he is sovereign in justly leaving other sinners in their lost condition. "On the part of the elect he would have us contemplate the mercy of God, and on the part of the reprobate to acknowledge his righteous judgment. . . . It may also . . . be noticed, that though Paul saw that this doctrine could not be touched on without exciting instant clamours and dreadful blasphemies, yet he freely and openly brought it forward."[18]

Again for Calvin this doctrine of reprobation is the unavoid-

---

[15]Ibid., on Rom. 9:16, 357ff.
[16]Calvin, *Institutes*, III, 24, 1, altered.
[17]Ibid., III, 24, 2, altered.
[18]Calvin, *Commentary on Romans*, on Rom. 9:14, 354ff., altered.

ably clear teaching of the Bible. The apostle Paul wrote (Rom. 9:10–13): ". . . when Rebekah had conceived children by one man, our forefather Isaac, though they were not yet born and had done nothing either good or bad—in order that God's purpose of election might continue, not because of works but because of him who calls—she was told, 'The older will serve the younger.' As it is written, 'Jacob I loved, but Esau I hated.'" Calvin taught this double predestination—election to eternal life and reprobation to damnation—because Paul taught it to show how God's mercy and his justice glorified God.

The life and actions of the reprobate confirm the justice of God's judgment: ". . . for all those external things, which lead to the blinding of the reprobate, are the instruments of his wrath; and Satan himself, who works inwardly with great power, is so far his minister, that he acts not, but by his command. . . . Paul teaches us, that the ruin of the wicked is not only foreseen by the Lord, but also ordained by his counsel and will."[19]

The doctrine of reprobation also makes clear that God is not frustrated in accomplishing his purposes. The apostasy of Judas (John 6) and the unbelief of part of Israel (Romans 9) does not mean that God has failed, but rather that God is working out his decree of reprobation.

Calvin acknowledges that questions remain about reprobation as well as election to life but again calls Christians to be content with what God has revealed without trying to find reasons known only to God himself. "But that Paul is silent as to the reason, why they are vessels appointed to destruction, is no matter of wonder. He indeed takes it as granted, according to what has been already said, that the reason is hid in the secret and inexplorable counsel of God; whose justice it behooves us rather to adore than scrutinize."[20]

Nevertheless Calvin insists that God's reprobating judgment is just and should lead all Christians to ever greater humil-

[19]Ibid., on Rom. 9:18, 362.
[20]Ibid., on Rom. 9:21, 368ff.

ity. Christians are not elect because they are better than the reprobate, but only because of the surprising and utterly gracious mercy of God.

PREDESTINATION AND CHRIST

Calvin insists that Christ, not speculation, must be at the center of the doctrine of predestination. Christians must seek Christ in the Bible, and only in Christ will Christians know their salvation and therefore their election:

> . . . if we seek the fatherly mercy and the propitious heart of God, our eyes must be directed to Christ, in whom alone the Father is well pleased. If we seek salvation, life, and the immortality of the heavenly kingdom, recourse must be had to no other, for he alone is the fountain of life, the anchor of salvation, and the heir of the kingdom of heaven. . . . The persons, therefore, whom God has adopted as his children, he is said to have chosen, not in themselves, but in his Christ. . . . But if we are chosen in him, we shall find no assurance of our election in ourselves, nor even in God the Father, considered alone, abstractly from the Son. Christ, therefore, is the mirror in which we must contemplate our election; and here we may do it with safety. . . . We have a testimony sufficiently clear and strong that if we have communion with Christ, we are written in the book of life.[21]

Christ Is the Foundational Evidence of Election

> Therefore, if we want to know whether God is concerned for our salvation, let us inquire whether he has committed us to Christ, whom he established as the only Savior of all his people.[22]

Christ Preserves His Own

> Now there is no doubt, that when Christ intercedes for all the elect, he prays for them the same as he did for Peter, that their faith may never fail. From this we conclude that they are beyond all danger of falling away, because the intercessions of the Son of

---

[21]Calvin, *Institutes*, III, 24, 5, altered.
[22]Ibid., III, 24, 6, altered.

God for their perseverance in piety have not been rejected. What did Christ intend we should learn from this, but confidence in our perpetual security, since we have once been introduced into the number of his people?[23]

And doubtless, as Christ was the only refuge in great extremities, no solid comfort could have been brought to miserable sinners, and such as saw God's wrath impending over them, except by setting Christ before their eyes.[24]

Christ Has Done All the Work to Save the Elect

Christ has been given to us for righteousness; whosoever obtrudes on God the righteousness of works, attempts to rob him of his office. And hence it appears that whenever men, under the empty pretence of being zealous for righteousness, put confidence in their works, they do in their furious madness carry on war with God himself. But how they stumble at Christ, who trust in their works, it is not difficult to understand; for except we own ourselves to be sinners, void and destitute of any righteousness of our own, we obscure the dignity of Christ, which consists in this, that to us all he is light, life, resurrection, righteousness, and healing.[25]

PREDESTINATION AND COVENANT

In later Reformed theology the doctrine of the covenants is developed in detail as part of the way in which Calvinists talk about God's plan of redemption and the importance of human history and actions. Almost all Calvinists will hold to a two-covenant theology—namely, the covenant of works with Adam and the covenant of grace for sinners. As Adam was promised life as the fruit of his obedience, so all mankind fell into sin as the fruit of his disobedience. God, to save a people for his name, then established a covenant of grace to save fallen Adam and all the elect. God ultimately saves his people through Christ who as the second

---

[23]Ibid., altered.
[24]Calvin, *Commentaries on Romans*, on Rom. 9:25, 372.
[25]Ibid., on Rom. 9:32, 379.

Adam wins life for his people by his obedience in life and in death. Reformed theology also recognizes that under the covenant of grace are several more specific covenants that give expression to the covenant of grace.

While Calvin himself does not develop these ideas fully or use them regularly in his theology, the roots of all these ideas are clearly present in Calvin. "For since Christ came to redeem us from the calamity into which Adam has fallen, and had precipitated all his posterity with him, we can see with so much clearness what we have in Christ, as by having what we have lost in Adam set before us."[26] Calvin acknowledges, as does the developed doctrine of the covenant of works, that the Law is a way to salvation when it is kept perfectly: "The law is indeed by itself, as it teaches us what righteousness is, the way to salvation: but our depravity and corruption prevent it from being in this respect of any advantage to us."[27]

For Calvin the promises of God flow from the covenants of God by which God has bound himself, and the covenants flow from election. No tension or problem exists here between election and covenant.

> As Paul has distinguished here between *covenants* and *promises*, we may observe this difference, that a covenant is that which is expressed in distinct and accustomed words, and contains a mutual stipulation, as that which was made with Abraham; but promises are what we meet with everywhere in Scripture; for when God had once made a covenant with his ancient people, he continued to offer, often by new promises, his favour to them. It hence follows, that promises are to be traced up to the covenant as to their true source; in the same manner the special helps of God, by which he testifies his love towards the faithful, may be said to flow from the true fountain of election.[28]

In particular Calvin recognized that some who were included

---

[26]Ibid., on Rom. 5:12, 111.
[27]Ibid., on Rom. 3:20, 133, altered.
[28]Ibid., on Rom. 9:4, 340.

in the external form of the covenant, whether in Israel or in the church, would not actually be saved under the covenant. In other words, the covenant is a broader category than election. "The statement is, that the promise was so given to Abraham and to his seed, that the inheritance did not belong to every seed without distinction; it hence follows that the defection of some does not prove that the covenant does not remain firm and valid. . . . The general election of the people of Israel is no hindrance, that God should not from them choose by his hidden counsel those whom he pleases."[29]

More specifically Calvin shows how individuals can be added to or removed from the covenant community without in any way affecting the immutability of election.

> But if it be asked respecting individuals, "How any one could be cut off from the grafting, and how, after excision, he could be grafted again,"—bear in mind, that there are three modes of insition [ingrafting], and two modes of excision. For instance, the children of the faithful are ingrafted, to whom the promise belongs according to the covenant made with the fathers; ingrafted are also they who indeed receive the seed of the gospel, but it strikes no root, or is choked before it brings any fruit; and thirdly, the elect are ingrafted, who are illuminated unto eternal life according to the immutable purpose of God. The first are cut off, when they refuse the promise given to their fathers, or do not receive it on account of ingratitude; the second are cut off, when the seed is withered and destroyed; and as the danger of this impends over all, with regard to their own nature, it must be allowed that this warning which Paul gives belongs in a certain way to the faithful, lest they indulge themselves in the sloth of the flesh.[30]

Here is a remarkable statement about the relationship of election and covenant.

For Calvin, predestination explains the origin of salvation in the eternal will of God. Election removes all human boasting and

---

[29]Ibid., on Rom. 9:6, 344ff.
[30]Ibid., on Rom. 11:22, 433ff.

gives all glory to God in salvation. The covenant helps explain God's action in history, shows how the history of redemption unfolds in the Bible, and underscores the importance of the institutions of the covenant of grace as the ways in which God accomplishes his purposes for his elect. Predestination as the foundation of salvation and the church is essential to confident assurance for Christians of God's blessing in their lives.

Covenant mercies and election can only be known from the Bible. Calvin recognizes the danger that awaits those who seek to investigate their election apart from the Word.

> Those who, in order to gain an assurance of their election, examine the eternal counsel of God apart from the Word, plunge themselves into a fatal abyss. . . . Those who investigate it in a regular and orderly manner as it is contained in the Word derive from such inquiry the benefit of peculiar consolation. Let this, therefore, be our way of our inquiry: to begin and end with the calling of God.[31]

---

[31]Calvin, *Institutes*, III, 24, 4, altered.

The Church, the City, and the Schools

Calvin longed to create a genuinely Christian society both in the hearts of individuals and in the outward forms of all Genevan life. Such an ideal was not new to Calvin. Since the conversion of Emperor Constantine to Christianity in the early fourth century, church and state in the ancient Roman world, in the Byzantine Empire, and in the medieval West had cooperated (and competed) with each other to create a Christian civilization. All the major Reformers remained committed to this task. This is not to say that they all had precisely the same goals or strategies, but the ideal of the state cooperating with and supporting the one true church remained. None of the Reformers could have anticipated that the division of the church resulting from the Reformation would contribute to the growing secularization of the West and the loss of the ideal of a unified Christian civilization. Calvin lived in a time when a secular state and a variety of Christian denominations were unthinkable.

DISCIPLINE IN THE CITY

For Calvin the ideal of a Christian society remained strong in Geneva. Calvin participated with the other ministers and the elders in the work of the Consistory to reform the moral life of the city. In cooperation with the city council, the Consistory tackled problems of drinking, dancing, and sexual immorality in the city. The council outlawed card playing and dancing in the city. (Calvin was not absolutely opposed to dancing but rejected the lascivious forms it had taken in Geneva.) Laws sought to reduce the amount of drinking in taverns and required a Bible to be placed in every tavern. Laws also restricted the wearing of extravagantly expensive clothing. Punishment could take a number of forms depending on the seriousness of the offense and the sincerity of the offender's penitence.

A number of these laws were not entirely new. Many reflected laws adopted in the Middle Ages, while others were adopted by the Protestant city council before Calvin came to Geneva. What was new was the serious effort to enforce these laws and ideals. The Consistory was a new institution in the city, and it was very serious in its effort to control public behavior. Later in the century when Reformed Christianity had spread to parts of the Netherlands, one Dutch opponent of the new faith captured the attitude of many of Calvin's detractors when he said, "Better the Spanish Inquisition than the Genevan Consistory."

Punishment could be severe indeed, although the most serious physical punishments were imposed by the civil courts, not by the church Consistory. For example, in 1547 Jacques Gruet publicly criticized Calvin and the ministers, actually placing a poster of protest on the pulpit in St. Pierre's. He was arrested and his home searched. There writings were found in which he rejected the idea of divine revelation and disparaged all laws. He also rejected the idea of the immortality of the soul. Such a free thinker was seen as a threat to the unity and stability of the city. Geneva, like most governments of Europe in the sixteenth century, believed such a crime deserved serious punishment. The civil government tortured Gruet, forcing him to confess, and condemned him to death by beheading, all in the course of a few weeks. Many moderns have criticized Calvin for his involvement in such actions, and certainly almost all modern Calvinists would reject coercion by the state to enforce true religion as unbiblical. Calvin certainly commended these actions even though he was not a part of the civil government. On these matters Calvin remained a medieval man and thought as most Europeans did then. Serious heresy was seen as a spiritual plague threatening the whole society and had to be quickly eradicated to prevent it from spreading.

In Geneva Calvin's opponents found a variety of ways to show their disapproval of this religious seriousness. Some named their dogs after Calvin; others composed little songs to criticize the ministers; some abbreviated his name from Calvin to Cain. Some, required by law to attend church services, shouted at him while he preached so that police had to be brought into church to keep order. Even then people showed their unhappiness with rude noises.

Calvin was frustrated but not surprised by such troubles. While he believed in a Christian society and in the value of outward conformity to true religion and moral behavior for the health of the state, he knew that such conformity did not guarantee internal faith and a truly Christian life. Calvin did not believe that he or those who would come after him would live in a golden age.

> . . . for though God now appears to the world in full light, yet very few there are who submit themselves to his word; and of this small number fewer still there are who sincerely and without any dissimulation embrace sound doctrine. We indeed see how great is their inconstancy and indifference. For they who pretend great zeal for a time very soon vanish and fall away. . . . We may also derive hence an admonition no less useful—not to regard ours as the golden age, because some portion of men profess the pure worship of God: for many, by no means wicked men, think, that almost all mortals are like angels, as soon as they testify in words their approbation of the gospel: and the sacred name of Reformation is at this day profaned, when anyone who shows as it were by a nod only that he is not wholly an enemy to the gospel, is immediately lauded as a person of extraordinary piety. Though then many show some regard for religion, let us yet know that among so large a number there are many hypocrites,

and that there is much chaff mixed with the wheat: and that our senses may not deceive us, we may see here, as in a mirror, how difficult it is to restore the world to the obedience of God, and utterly to root up all corruptions, though idols may be taken away and superstitions be abolished.[1]

Repeatedly in his writings Calvin indicated that he thought only one in ten Genevans was really committed to true religion. On his bad days he would say that not one in one hundred was a true Christian.

The opposition to Calvin also took serious political forms, and from 1541 to 1555 political support for Calvin waxed and waned. From 1541 to 1546 Calvin's supporters were dominant in the government, but from 1547 to 1553 his supporters and opponents were very evenly divided. During this period from time to time Calvin expected that he might well be exiled again.

In August 1553 an even more difficult time for Calvin began when Michael Servetus (1511–1553) arrived in Geneva. He was a Spanish physician who was an old theological enemy of Calvin. As early as the 1530s Servetus had written a book rejecting the Christian doctrine of the Trinity. He was part of a small movement in the sixteenth century that concluded that the Trinity was another false doctrine imposed on Christians by the Roman Church. Servetus argued that Jesus was not divine and was not the eternal Son of God.

Already in the 1530s Calvin tried to arrange a meeting with Servetus so he could win him from his heresy. Calvin went to the meeting that had been arranged, but Servetus did not show up. Still Servetus continued to write against the Trinity, which was a very dangerous thing to do. Almost anywhere in Europe if he had been denounced to the authorities, he would have been arrested and executed. But he wrote anonymously and often moved from place to place.

In the mid-1540s Calvin again corresponded with Servetus

---

[1]John Calvin, *Commentary on the Twelve Minor Prophets*, Vol. 4 (Grand Rapids, MI: Baker, 1979), on Zeph. 1:2–3, 187 (originally published in 1559).

to try to persuade him of the error of his ways. When that effort failed, Calvin warned Servetus that the doctrine he was espousing was lethal to his own soul and dangerous to the Christian community and would lead to his execution if arrested.

Early in 1553 Servetus published yet another work attacking the Trinity entitled *Restitution of the Christian Religion*. The title was a clear and deliberate attack on Calvin and his *Institutes*. After this work appeared, Servetus was arrested by Roman Catholic authorities in southern France. He managed to escape but was condemned *in absentia* for his heresy and would have been executed had he been captured in France. As Servetus knew, for over a thousand years Christian governments had judged anti-trinitarianism to be a capital offense.

Servetus arrived in Geneva in August 1553, probably intending to cause trouble for Calvin. He was recognized, denounced, and arrested as a notorious heretic. Calvin insisted that he be placed on trial for his heresy.

The city council saw the trial of Servetus as a possible opportunity to embarrass Calvin; yet they knew they could not side with Servetus. So they decided to drag out the trial as a way to harass Calvin. They delayed the trial by writing various governments in Switzerland and elsewhere in Europe seeking advice on how Servetus should be treated. Almost all the letters that came back had the same advice: he must be condemned for his terrible heresy and executed.

In October the trial finally took place. Members of the city council served as judges, and Calvin functioned as the chief prosecutor. Servetus was condemned and ordered to be executed by burning at the stake, the traditional medieval punishment for heresy. Calvin and the other ministers pled that the punishment should be changed to beheading, a much quicker and less painful form of execution. The city council refused. Justice moved swiftly in those days: he was tried on October 20, condemned on October 21, and executed on October 26.

Calvin and the other ministers continued to appeal to Servetus to repent right up to the time of his execution, but Servetus adamantly maintained his heresy. His dying words were, "Jesus, son of the eternal God, have mercy on me." By those words Servetus maintained even in the flames that Jesus was not himself eternal God.

Through the centuries since this execution Calvin has been frequently portrayed as severe, judgmental, intolerant, and violent. He has been represented as a great persecutor. In fact, Calvin's attitude toward punishing heretics was quite typical in the sixteenth century. However barbaric such views may seem today, the vast majority of Europeans would have agreed with Calvin in his day. In fact, there were fewer executions for heresy in Geneva than in many parts of Europe.

The execution of Servetus was highlighted as a sign of Calvin's cruelty in one of the first biographies of Calvin, written in 1577 (thirteen years after Calvin's death) by one of Calvin's old enemies, Jerome Bolsec. Bolsec had returned to the Roman Catholic Church and wrote a biography filled with recriminations and lies. Some of his charges against Calvin were ridiculous, for example, accusing Calvin of being both a homosexual and a womanizer. The lies of Bolsec led Theodore Beza, Calvin's friend and fellow minister, to write in Calvin's defense his own valuable biography of Calvin.

Calvin's struggles with city leaders continued in 1554 once again over the old issue of church discipline. One of the leading men of the city was excommunicated, and the question of the church's authority was raised again. Everyone looked to the elections of February 1555 to see how citizens would react to this latest struggle. In that election those supporting Calvin and a disciplined church won overwhelmingly. If 1553 was the low point for Calvin politically in Geneva, 1555 was the high point. From that election until the time of his death in 1564, Calvin's life in Geneva became secure and peaceful. No serious problems arose between Calvin and the city council from that time forward.

Over the years the political tensions in Geneva were at times exacerbated for Calvin by the steady stream of religious refugees flowing into the city. The population of the city would about double in the time that Calvin lived there. Old inhabitants saw the new refugees as a threat to their control, especially since almost all the refugees were strong followers of Calvin. Some of the refugees were such distinguished people that eventually they had to be admitted to citizenship in the city. By 1555 the changed character of the city at last brought Calvin a measure of reliable political support.

CALVIN AND THE SCHOOLS

Calvin ultimately realized his goal of establishing in Geneva schools that offered education at all levels and met the diverse needs of the city, the church, and individual citizens. Calvin's most basic concern was for the education of ministers to serve the church. Already in the draft ecclesiastical articles of 1541 Calvin writes of four orders in the church. Calvin is following the teaching of Martin Bucer and the practice of the Reformed church in Strassburg. Chapter 5 of this study examined Calvin's thought about ministers, elders, and deacons. The fourth office, doctors (or teachers), relates particularly to the schools. Of these doctors Calvin writes: "The office proper to doctors is the instruction of the faithful in true doctrine, in order that the purity of the Gospel be not corrupted either by ignorance or by evil opinions. . . . So to use a more intelligible word, we will call this the order of the schools."[2] He expresses a desire that the school at the level of ministerial education have a doctor of Old Testament and another of New Testament to lecture in theology.

Calvin recognized that such ministerial education had to build on basic university studies: "But because it is only possible to profit from such lectures [in theology] if first one is instructed in the languages and humanities, and also because it is necessary to raise offspring for time to come, in order not to leave the Church deserted to our children, a college should be instituted

---

[2]*Calvin: Theological Treatises*, "Draft Ecclesiastical Ordinances," trans. J.K.S. Reid (Philadelphia: Westminster, 1954), 62.

for instructing children to prepare them for the ministry as well as for civil government."[3] The state as well as the church needed educated citizens.

In turn university studies rested on earlier education beginning around age seven. While the structure of the levels of education basically follows the pattern traditional in the Middle Ages, the curriculum and goals of education were greatly revised under the influence of the Renaissance and Reformation. Reformation goals aimed at teaching as many as possible in society to read so that they could know the Bible. Renaissance curriculum stressed the importance of clear thinking and writing as well as the skill for the careful reading of texts. The early years of the curriculum of the Genevan schools focused on reading, writing, and the study of French, Latin, and Greek.

The education in Geneva was decidedly confessional. As professors were to subscribe to the confession of Geneva, students were to swear to a long oath—about twenty-one paragraphs—summarizing the doctrinal position of the city and church. The oath begins: "I affirm that I wish to follow and hold the doctrine of the faith as it is contained in the catechism of this church, and that I subject myself also to the discipline established there, and that I do not adhere to or agree with any sects which might trouble the peace and unity which God has put here according to his Word."[4]

The great aim of all this education was, first, an educated laity to read and understand the Bible and, second, an educated ministry. Those who graduated from the Academy of Geneva to become ministers often joked that their diploma was their death certificate because so many would become first preachers and then martyrs in France. In time the Reformed schools in Geneva and elsewhere in Europe would achieve their educational goals. Literacy would become widespread in Reformed countries, and a remarkable body of well-educated ministers would serve the churches.

---

[3]Ibid., 63.
[4]Translated from S. Stelling-Michaud, *Le Livre du Recteur de l'Academie de Geneve (1559–1878)* (Geneva: E. Droz, 1959), 74.

In the short run, however, there was a serious shortage of ministers in Geneva and in many other parts of Reformed Europe. The shortage in Geneva was particularly serious between 1541 and 1546. From 1546 on, the Genevan church was served with a very strong and united group of ministers, although problems continued. Low salaries were especially a problem as ministers now usually had families that needed to be supported. Also the Genevan church had the problem that all its ministers were French rather than native Genevans, which meant that in times of difficulty some in the city would accuse the ministers of being trouble-making foreigners.

Before 1559 when the Academy of Geneva was fully established as a college for ministers, Calvin lectured informally to help prepare students for the ministry. Theodore Beza joined Calvin in Geneva in 1558, leaving behind the troubles of Lausanne, and in 1559 Beza was named rector of the Genevan Academy.

The education and preparation of ministers in Geneva included careful academic preparation, thorough examination of their doctrinal commitments and moral character, and practical preparation through serving in rural churches. The Reformed ministers became a remarkable group of dedicated and qualified men who preached, taught, and pastored the church with great skill and faithfulness.

CALVIN AS
PASTORAL COUNSELOR

C alvin was a counselor, in the widest sense, in all that he did and wrote for the church. His ministry in all its parts was designed to direct, encourage, and rebuke Christians according to their needs. Through his theology and commentaries, through his sermons and letters, Calvin counseled Christians and churches in Geneva and throughout Europe.

PROVIDENCE AND THE *INSTITUTES*

One of the foundations of all Calvin's counsel to Christians in their varying needs is his profound teaching on providence. All his advice and direction—whether to faith, hope, or love, whether to patience or intense action—rest at least in part on his understanding of God's providential care for his people. His teaching on providence can be found especially in his *Institutes* and in his commentaries.

In the early editions of the *Institutes* Calvin discussed providence and predestination together. As God governs all things by his will (providence), so he particularly governs the salvation of his elect (predestination). The two do indeed fit together. But in the 1559 *Institutes* Calvin separates the two, discussing providence in Book I in relation to God the Father and discussing predestination in Book III as the source of the Spirit's gift of faith.

Calvin saw this separation as a way to make the value of predestination to the Christian clearer and more intimately related to the matters of salvation.

In Book I of the 1559 *Institutes* Calvin devotes three chapters to providence (Chapters 16–18), the longest of which he entitled "The Proper Application of This Doctrine to Render It Useful to Us" (Chapter 17). For Calvin the truth of providence is not simply an abstract or speculative idea about the sovereignty of God but a very practical reality that every Christian needs to understand and embrace. Christians need this doctrine because life often seems meaningless and futile: "Human life is beset by innumerable evils, and threatened with a thousand deaths. . . . Amid these difficulties, must not man be most miserable, who is half dead while he lives, and is dispirited and alarmed as though he had a sword perpetually hanging over his neck?"[1] Apart from a knowledge of God's care, life and death are frightening and pointless.

After reminding his readers of the great assurance of the saints in the Bible in the face of their troubles, he asks, "How is it that their security remains unshaken, while the world appears to be revolving at random, but because they know that the Lord is everywhere at work and because they trust that his work is beneficial for them?"[2] Calvin stresses that the Lord is everywhere at work in this world.

God not only works but is absolutely sovereign over all things that come to pass: ". . . all events are governed by the secret counsel of God."[3] This governance is personal and active: "And, indeed, God asserts that he is omnipotent and calls us to acknowledge this attribute: not such as the Sophists imagine— vain, idle, and almost asleep, but vigilant, effective, active, engaged in ceaseless activity."[4] All creatures are governed in all that they do. God "regulates all things in such a manner that

---

[1] John Calvin, *Institutes*, I, 17, 10, altered.
[2] Ibid., I, 17, 11, altered.
[3] Ibid., I, 16, 2.
[4] Ibid., I, 16, 3, altered.

nothing happens except according to his counsel."[5] No accident occurs in God's universe: ". . . there can be no such thing as fortuitous chance."[6] His governance extends to the smallest details: ". . . not a drop of rain falls except at the express command of God."[7]

While God is sovereign over all things, Calvin insists that this doctrine of providence does not make God the author of or guilty for evil in the world. Calvin at length shows how this can be true. While he discusses this subject philosophically at times, his main interest is in the religious significance of this doctrine as it is presented in the Bible. He wants to reassure Christians that God is both sovereign and not the author of evil. Tellingly he borrows an analogy from Augustine to show briefly how this can be: "And from where, I ask, comes the fetid smell of a carcass, which has been putrefied and laid open by the heat of the sun? It is visible to all that it is stirred up by the sun's rays; yet no person on this account says that the rays stink."[8] God does not create evil, but by his action and governance he causes it to manifest itself, and he overcomes it.

Even more importantly for the believer, Calvin stresses that the Lord's work is always for the welfare of his people. In God's sovereign control of all things, he ever has a particular concern for his own. "The vigilance of the particular providence of God for the safety of the faithful is attested by numerous and very remarkable promises."[9] This truth is one of the most important teachings of the Bible. "Moreover, the principal purpose of the biblical histories is to teach us that the Lord so carefully defends the ways of the saints that they may not even 'dash their foot against a stone.'"[10]

Calvin passionately rejects any notion that this doctrine of providence would produce passivity or fatalism in Christians who

---

[5]Ibid., altered.
[6]Ibid., I, 16, 4, altered.
[7]Ibid., I, 16, 5, altered.
[8]Ibid., I, 17, 5, altered.
[9]Ibid., I, 17, 6, altered.
[10]Ibid., altered.

accept this truth.[11] Indeed, in Calvin himself and in his followers diligent activity was to be found, to the consternation of many who opposed them. Real Calvinists have never been fatalists or passive in their living.

For Calvin this doctrine brings the greatest blessings to the believer: "The necessary consequences of this knowledge are, gratitude in prosperity, patience in adversity, and a wonderful security respecting the future."[12] So he summarizes: ". . . you will easily perceive on examination that ignorance of providence is the greatest of miseries; but that the knowledge of it is attended with the highest happiness."[13] Christians live with the assurance that the sovereign God is their Father for the sake of Christ and directs all things for their good.

PROVIDENCE AND THE PSALTER

Calvin presents a systematic exposition of the doctrine of providence in his *Institutes*. Also, in his various works on the book of Psalms he follows the Psalter in a very personal and experiential expression of his understanding of providence. The Psalms were very important to Calvin, and he returned to them again and again in his ministry.

In 1557 Calvin published his large commentary on the book of Psalms. In the English translation this commentary runs to five substantial volumes. It reflects a life lived with the Psalter. He loved the Psalms: he knew them, studied them, wrote on them, preached them, and sang them. As early as 1539, while in Strassburg, he produced a Psalter with a few metrical psalms for singing. Throughout his career he encouraged poets to versify psalms for singing and encouraged composers to prepare appropriate melodies.

Calvin also showed his interest in the Psalms by preaching from them. He preached through the entire book of Psalms—off and on—from 1545 to 1560. Only for the Psalms did Calvin

---

[11]Ibid., I, 17, 9.
[12]Ibid., I, 17, 7.
[13]Ibid., I, 17, 11, altered.

break his regular pattern of preaching only from the New Testament on Sundays. Clearly they were close to his heart and of great spiritual significance for him and for the church.

He also used the Psalms in his teaching work. He began lecturing on the Psalms to the schoolboys of the Genevan Academy in 1552. He lectured or preached on the Psalms to the Friday gathering of ministers from 1555 to 1559.

Calvin was drawn to the Psalms, as he makes clear in the Preface to the commentary, because of his strong identification with the emotions of David expressed in these poems. He believed that the value of these poems was not just for himself but for all Christians. The Psalms teach all to know and honor God: ". . . there is no other book in which we are more perfectly taught the right manner of praising God, or in which we are more powerfully stirred up to the performance of this religious exercise."[14]

The Psalms show that Christians are to offer praise and prayer to God with all the emotions evoked from the various circumstances of life. Calvin sees the Psalter as "'An Anatomy of all the Parts of the Soul;' for there is not an emotion of which any one can be conscious that is not here represented as in a mirror. Or rather, the fears, doubts, hopes, cares, perplexities, in short, all the distracting emotions with which the minds of men are wont to be agitated."[15] In particular for Calvin the Psalms teach the vital lesson that the Christian will suffer for his Lord in this life: ". . . they will principally teach and train us to bear the cross."[16] In their sufferings the Psalms will provide encouragement, teaching "true believers with their whole hearts confidently to look to him for help in all their necessities."[17]

In the course of his commentary Calvin gives strong expression to various aspects of the doctrine of providence. Five themes about providence recur in Calvin's exposition of the Psalms.

First, he recognizes God's power as the active governor of

---

[14]John Calvin, *Commentary on the Psalms*, Vol. 1 (Grand Rapids, MI: Baker, 1979), xxxviii–xxxix.
[15]Ibid., xxxvii.
[16]Ibid., xxxix.
[17]Ibid.

the world: "He gives us to understand by this word, that heaven is not a palace in which God remains idle and indulges in pleasures, as the Epicureans dream, but a royal court, from which he exercises his government over all parts of the world. If he has erected his throne, therefore, in the sanctuary of heaven, in order to govern the universe, it follows that he in no wise neglects the affairs of earth, but governs them with the highest reason and wisdom."[18]

Second, this active power should lead all his creatures to honor him as God: "As God by his providence preserves the world, the power of his government is alike extended to all, so that he ought to be worshipped by all, even as he also shows to all men, without exception, the fatherly care he has about them."[19]

Third, he teaches that in his governance of the world God always acts as the loving Father of his people: "By *the face of God*, must be meant the fatherly care and providence which he extends to his people. So numerous are the dangers which surround us, that we could not stand a single moment, if his eye did not watch over our preservation. But the true security for a happy life lies in being persuaded that we are under divine government."[20]

This fatherly care of God does not mean that his people will not suffer.

> . . . we are here warned that the guardianship of God does not secure us from being sometimes exercised with the cross and afflictions, and that therefore the faithful ought not to promise themselves a delicate and easy life in this world, it being enough for them not to be abandoned of God when they stand in need of his help. Their heavenly Father, it is true, loves them most tenderly, but he will have them awakened by the cross, lest they should give themselves too much to the pleasures of the flesh. If, therefore, we embrace this doctrine, although we may happen to be oppressed by the tyranny of the wicked, we will wait

---

[18]Ibid., on Ps. 33:13.
[19]Ibid., on Ps. 24:1.
[20]Ibid., on Ps. 62.

patiently till God either break their sceptre, or shake it out of their hands.[21]

Fourth, assurance in God's providence will cause Christians to grow in faith in Christ and in confident living for him.

> Besides, the joy here mentioned arises from this, that there is nothing more calculated to increase our faith, than the knowledge of the providence of God; because without it, we would be harassed with doubts and fears, being uncertain whether or not the world was governed by chance. For this reason, it follows that those who aim at the subversion of this doctrine, depriving the children of God of true comfort, and vexing their minds by unsettling their faith, forge for themselves a hell upon earth. For what can be more awfully tormenting than to be constantly racked with doubt and anxiety? And we will never be able to arrive at a calm state of mind until we are taught to repose with implicit confidence in the providence of God.[22]

Fifth, knowing that God directs all things will lead his people to more frequent and heartfelt prayer. "Were they to reflect on the judgments of God, they would at once perceive that there was nothing like chance or fortune in the government of the world. Moreover, until men are persuaded that all their troubles come upon them by the appointment of God, it will never come into their minds to supplicate him for deliverance."[23]

The Psalms teach Christians to combine, meditating on the promises and providences of God with prayer.

> In this verse, as we have often seen to be the case in other places, the people of God intermingle meditations with their prayers, thereby to acquire renewed vigour to their faith, and to stir up themselves to greater earnestness in the duty of prayer. We know how difficult it is to rise above all doubts, and boldly persevere in a free and unrestrained course of prayer. Here, then, the faithful call to remembrance the proofs of God's mercy and working,

---

[21]Ibid., on Ps. 125:3.
[22]Ibid., on Ps. 107:42.
[23]Ibid., on Ps. 107:11.

by which he certified, through a continued series of ages, that he was the King and Protector of the people whom he had chosen. By this example we are taught, that as it is not enough to pray with the lips unless we also pray in faith, we ought always to remember the benefits by which God has given a confirmation of his fatherly love towards us, and should regard them as so many testimonies of his electing love.[24]

Prayer was a matter of great concern for Calvin. The Psalter taught the church the necessity, content, and blessing of prayer. He stressed the importance of prayer for Christians in his commentary. Also in the 1559 *Institutes* Calvin wrote a chapter on prayer (Book III, Chapter 20) that is a classic exposition of the biblical teaching on prayer. In that one chapter he gives more space to prayer than to predestination in the *Institutes*, a fact that should surely cause some to reconsider easy stereotypes of Calvin's religion.

In his preface to his commentary on the Psalms, Calvin makes a most remarkable statement about providence that goes to the very heart and soul of the religion he embraces. He writes that knowing the Psalter will teach Christians to suffer for God so that "we renounce the guidance of our own affections, and submit ourselves entirely to God, leaving him to govern us, and to dispose our life according to his will, so that the afflictions which are the bitterest and most severe to our nature, become sweet to us, because they proceed from him."[25] The bitterest afflictions of this life can be sweet when Christians know that they come from God, serve his purposes, and ultimately contribute to their good. Calvin himself had and encouraged in his followers a truly astounding daily confidence in God and his ways.

PROVIDENCE AND CALVIN'S LETTERS

Calvin applied his doctrine of providence in the counseling that he did for the people of God. He was a particularly personal and

---

[24]Ibid., on Ps. 107:12.
[25]Ibid., Preface, xxxix.

pointed counselor in his letters. During his ministry he wrote over twelve hundred letters to friends, acquaintances, churches, and even strangers. He wrote on great political issues of his day, on theology, on church conflicts, and often on personal problems.

Calvin often wrote his letters in haste and at times found the appeals to him for advice burdensome. He gave vent to his frustrations about letters in a letter to Bullinger: ". . . indeed I am so much exhausted by constant writing, and so greatly broken down by fatigue, that I frequently feel an almost positive aversion to writing a letter. Would that others had as much of your moderation as would enable them to cultivate a sincere friendship at the expense of less writing. Our French friends oppress me in this way beyond all consideration. It so happens, that by continually apologizing, I am getting myself suspected of indolence by my particular friends."[26] Still he continued to write voluminously.

To the Sick and Grieving

Some of his letters offer encouragement to the sick. For example, Calvin, who had himself been recently ill, wrote to the recently recovered Madame de Coligny, the wife of the Admiral of France who was one of the most important and faithful leaders of the Reformed in France, on August 5, 1563:

> It is certain that all diseases ought not only to humble us in setting before our eyes our frailty, but also cause us to look into ourselves, that having recognized our own poverty we may place all our trust in his mercy. They should, moreover, serve us for medicines to purge us from worldly affections, and retrench [remove] what is superfluous in us, and since they are to us the messengers of death, we ought to learn to have one foot raised to take our departure when it shall please God. Nevertheless, he lets us taste of his bounty as often as he delivers us from them. . . . And thus take courage, so much the more to give yourself up to

---

[26]John Calvin, *Selected Works*, Vol. 5, 1551, ed. H. Beveridge and J. Bonnet (Grand Rapids, MI: Baker, 1983), 304ff.

his service, as you do well to consider that it is to that end he has
reserved you.[27]

Other letters express consolation to those who are mourning.
For example, he wrote movingly to Richard Vauville, pastor of
the French Reformed Church in Frankfurt, on the death of his
wife, in November 1555:

> How deep a wound the death of your wife must have inflicted on
> your heart, I judge from my own feelings. For I recollect how dif-
> ficult it was for me seven years ago to get over a similar sorrow.
> But as you know perfectly well, what are the suitable remedies
> for alleviating an excessive sorrow, I have nothing else to do than
> to remind you to summon them to your aid. Among other things,
> this is no mean source of consolation . . . that you lived with
> a wife of such disposition, that you will willingly renew your
> fellowship with her when you shall be called out of this world.
> Then an example of dying piously was offered to you by the
> companion of your life. . . . As, however, our principal motive of
> consolation consists in this, that by the admirable providence of
> God, the things we consider adverse, contribute to our salvation,
> and that we are separated in the world only that we may be once
> more reunited in his celestial kingdom, in this you will from your
> piety acquiesce.[28]

To Those with Theological Questions

In his letters Calvin frequently answered theological questions
put to him by friends and strangers. A particularly interesting
example of such theological advice given in a very difficult situation is found in one of his letters written late in life to Renee of
France, the Duchess of Ferrara. She was a great noblewoman, the
daughter of King Louis XII of France. Calvin had corresponded
with her over many years, and her devotion to the Reformed
cause was strong. His letter of January 24, 1564 was clearly in
response to a letter of hers in which she expressed great distress

---

[27] Ibid., Vol. 7, 331ff.
[28] Ibid., Vol. 6, 236.

about the ways in which some Reformed ministers had spoken of her son-in-law, the Duke of Guise, after his death. The Duke of Guise had been a notorious persecutor of the Reformed church and had often been bitterly criticized by many Reformed leaders. Calvin urges her and others to moderation—to be neither too hard nor too soft. She complained to Calvin that someone (probably a minister) had declared his hatred of the Duke of Guise that she thought contrary to the character of the gospel. She noted that the critic had defended his strong words by appealing to the example of David in the Psalms. The Duchess suggested that perhaps some of David's sentiments were not appropriate for Christians in the New Covenant.

Calvin's reply is remarkable:

> Respecting what I had alleged to you that David teaches us by his example to hate the enemies of God, you reply that it was only from the rigor of the law, that it was permitted to hate enemies. Now, Madame, this gloss would lead to the overthrowing of the whole Scriptures, and for that reason we should shun it as we would a deadly plague. For we see that David surpassed in kindness of character the best of those that would be found in our days. Thus when he protests that he has wept and in secret shed tears for those who were plotting his death, we see that his hatred consisted in mourning for their death, that he was as meek-spirited as could possibly be desired. But when he says he holds the reprobate in mortal aversion, it cannot be doubted that he glories in an upright, pure, and well-regulated zeal, for which three things are requisite: first, that we should have no regard for ourselves nor our private interests; next, that we should possess prudence and discretion not to judge at random; and finally, that we observe moderation not to exceed the bounds of our calling.[29]

Clearly Calvin will not allow the kind of divide between Old and New Testaments suggested by the Duchess.

Indeed Calvin insists that the honor of God requires that

---

[29]Ibid., Vol. 7, 353, altered.

Christians at times speak strongly against God's enemies: "Nay, St. John, of whom you have retained nothing but the word love, clearly shows that we ought not, under show of an affection for men, become indifferent to the duty we owe to the honor of God and the preservation of his church."[30]

Calvin then expounds on the proper Christian concern for a persecutor of the church. About the Duke of Guise, Calvin writes: "For my own part, though I have often prayed God to show him mercy, yet it is certain I have often desired that God should lay his hand on him in order to deliver out of his hands the poor church, unless it pleased God to convert him. So I may protest that before the war, I had but to give my consent to have had him exterminated by those men of prompt and ready execution. To pronounce that he is damned, however, is to go too far, unless one had some certain and infallible mark of his reprobation."[31] So Calvin shows that he prayed for and even protected the Duke and believes that Christians ought not claim to judge the final state of his soul.

While strong language such as David's is legitimate to the Christian, Calvin argues that however much Christians criticize God's enemies, they still must seek to love them as individuals: ". . . we are all agreed, that in order to be recognized as children of God, it is proper for us to conform ourselves to his example, striving to do good to those who are unworthy of it, just as he causes his sun to shine on the evil and the good. Thus hatred and Christianity are things incompatible. I mean hatred towards persons—in opposition to the love we owe them. On the contrary we are to wish and even procure their good; and to labor, as much as in us lies, to maintain peace and concord with all men."[32]

Calvin expresses the point he is making to the Duchess in a brief form in his commentary on the Gospel of John: "We ought to pray that this man, and that man, and every man, may be saved, and thus include the whole human race, because we can-

---

[30]Ibid., Vol. 7, 354, altered.
[31]Ibid.
[32]Ibid., Vol. 7, 357, altered.

not yet distinguish the elect from the reprobate; and yet, while we desire the coming of the kingdom of God, we likewise pray that God may destroy his enemies."[33] Christians both pray for their enemies' conversion and at the same time pray for the destruction of all that opposes God at last.

To the Persecuted

Calvin also wrote letters, sermons, and treatises for the persecuted. John Calvin was well acquainted with persecution. He was himself an exile to Geneva from France. He followed the course of religious persecution closely, especially in France. He raised money for the suffering, commenting, "For though money is not readily to be found in these parts, I shall assuredly so bestir myself, should I be obliged to pawn my head and feet, that it will be found forthcoming here."[34] Calvin included prayers for the persecuted in the regular intercessory prayers during Sunday morning worship in Geneva.

> In a particular manner we commend to you our unhappy brothers who live dispersed under the tyranny of Antichrist, and deprived of the liberty of openly calling upon your name, and who have either been cast into prison or are oppressed by the enemies of the gospel in any other way, that you would grant, O most kind Father, to support them by the strength of your Spirit, so that they may never despair, but constantly persevere in your holy calling; that you would be pleased to stretch out your hand to them, as you know to be best for them, to comfort them in their adversity, and taking them under your protection, defend them from the ravening wolves; finally, fill them with all the gifts of your Spirit, that their life and death may both tend to your glory.[35]

This intercession was added to the regular prayers of the church in 1558.

---

[33]John Calvin, *Commentary on the Gospel According to John*, Vol. 2 (Grand Rapids, MI: Baker, 1979), 172.
[34]Ibid., 1557, 367.
[35]Ibid., "Form of Prayers," Vol. 2, 103, altered.

Calvin felt a great pastoral responsibility to the persecuted and so wrote several treatises[36] and many letters of spiritual counsel to those facing persecution. Calvin wrote out of a great concern that the Reformed in France might remain faithful, and especially that they might not compromise with the idolatrous ceremonies of the Roman Church.[37] For Calvin the Roman Mass in particular was to be avoided as "an unbearable blasphemy," both "cursed and execrable."[38] Yet not only the Mass[39] but any apparent participation in the idolatry of Roman worship must be shunned.[40] Calvin wrote, ". . . as before God we ought to manifest our detestation of idolatry, so also before men, we ought to abstain from whatsoever may make it appear that we approve thereof."[41] Calvin's call for purity in worship reflected the great importance that he placed on worship. He argued that ". . . to perform any act of idolatry, in order to gain the favour of man, is more to be shunned than death in its most fearful form."[42]

In the face of Roman Catholic governments and inquisitions determined to enforce conformity to the Roman Catholic faith, Calvin's uncompromising advice was demanding, and he knew it. Yet Calvin insisted that only two options were available to the true Christian—either flight from persecution or faithful enduring without compromise in the midst of persecution and suffering. He praised exiles: "You now give a bright example of the sincerity of your faith, in preferring even exile to perfidious dissimulation."[43]

In 1546 Calvin wrote to Madame de Bude, widow of Guillaume Bude, the greatest French Renaissance scholar. She

---

[36]See Carlos M. N. Eire, *War Against the Idols: The Reformation of Worship from Erasmus to Calvin* (Cambridge: Cambridge University Press, 1986), 240f. for a discussion of those treatises.
[37]For an excellent discussion of Calvin's views of the idolatry of Roman ceremonies, see ibid., 195–233.
[38]*Selected Works*, Vol. 4, 1541, 300, 302.
[39]Ibid., Vol. 6, 1554, 44ff.
[40]Ibid., 31.
[41]Ibid., Vol. 5, 1548, 179.
[42]Ibid., "On Shunning the Unlawful Rites of the Ungodly, and Preserving the Purity of the Christian Religion," Vol. 3, 1537, 370.
[43]Ibid., Vol. 5, 1549, 208.

had embraced the Reformed faith and believed that she should move to Geneva so she could practice her religion without the restraints that she faced in France. Calvin encouraged her to be faithful and thought the move to Geneva a good idea if she was not ready for martyrdom. She had asked if he could assure her of peace in Geneva. Calvin in his letter wrote in response to this last concern, "You will ask me if, being come hither, you shall always have assured repose. I confess that you will not; for while we are in this world, it is fitting that we should be like birds upon the branch. So it has pleased God, and it is good for us."[44] In this particularly vivid image—"birds upon the branch"—Calvin expressed the attitude to this present life that Christians need to cultivate.

Calvin knew, however, that many could not or would not become religious refugees. To those actually liable to persecution and death he wrote with passion to urge faithfulness: "Above all . . . under the tyranny of antichrist, if a man will live like a Christian, he must by continual training learn to die, so that no difficulty plead an excuse for him when the honour of his God is in question."[45] There must be no return to false religion: "What a shame it will be, if after having separated yourselves from the defilement and pollutions of Papal idolatry, we should return to wallow a second time therein, and become doubly abominable in the sight of God."[46]

His letters particularly seek to build up faith in those experiencing persecution. In the first place Calvin recognizes that faithfulness does not come naturally. Living for Christ is always difficult: ". . . if I would live to Christ, this world must be to me a scene of trial and vexation: the present life is appointed as the field of conflict."[47] The theme of conflict is often presented by Calvin in military language. The Christian is "called to combat."[48]

Calvin saw two different enemies against whom the Christian

[44]Ibid., 91.
[45]Ibid., Vol. 6, 1554, 22ff.
[46]Ibid., Vol. 7, 1559, 53.
[47]Ibid., Vol. 4, 1540, 211.
[48]Ibid., Vol. 6, 1557, 384.

had to be armed for battle. The obvious enemy was the persecutor of true religion.[49] But more frequently Calvin presented the great enemy as the Christian's own flesh. He wrote:

> But the capital point is that instead of indulging this weakness we should seek to shake it off and be reanimated by the Spirit of God. I say then that nothing is more opposite to Christianity, of which we make a profession, than that when the Son of God our captain calls us to the combat, we should be not only cold and fainthearted, but seized with such consternation as to desert his standard. Let us then strive against our flesh, seeing that it is our greatest enemy, and that we may obtain pardon of God let us not pardon ourselves, but rather let us be our own judges to condemn ourselves.[50]

The internal warfare against weakness and fear is a greater danger for the Christian than the executioner. If the weakness of the flesh is overcome, then any external enemy can be faced.

In the second place, Calvin specified the sources of strength for battle from which the Christian could find help in the struggle. The ultimate source was the grace of God, but Calvin reminded his readers again and again that the Lord ministers his grace through specific, appointed means. Repeatedly Calvin called the persecuted to prayer and reading and hearing the Scriptures as the key to fortifying the soul against suffering. Calvin wrote:

> May the reliance which God commands us to have in his grace and in his strength always be to you an impregnable fortress; and for the holding fast the assurance of his help, may you be careful to walk in his fear, although, when we have made it our whole study to serve him, we must always come back to this conclusion, of asking pardon for our shortcomings. And inasmuch as you know well from experience how frail we are, be ever diligent to continue in the practice which you have established, of prayer and hearing of the holy word, to exercise you, and to sharpen and confirm you more and more.[51]

---

[49]For example, ibid., 365.
[50]Ibid., Vol. 7, 1559, 82ff.
[51]Ibid., Vol. 5, 1547, 131.

From the Scriptures the Christian needs both the encouragement of the promises of God and the warnings and proddings of the exhortations. This proper use of the Scriptures is itself a struggle. Calvin wrote:

> Many are overcome, because they allow their zeal to grow cold, and run off in self-flattery. Others, on the contrary, become so alarmed when they do not find in themselves the strength they wish, that they get confused, and give up the struggle altogether. What then is to be done? Arouse yourself to meditate, as much upon the promises of God, which ought to serve as ladders to raise us up to heaven, and make us despise this transitory and fading life, as upon the threatenings, which may well induce us to fear his judgments. When you do not feel your heart moved as it ought to be, have recourse, as to a special remedy, to diligently seeking the aid of him without whom we can do nothing. In the meantime, strive to your utmost, blaming coldness and weakness, until you can perceive that there is some amendment. And in regard to this, great caution is required so as to hold a middle course, namely, to groan unceasingly, and even to woo yourself to sadness and dissatisfaction with your condition, and to such a sense of misery as that you may have no rest; without, at the same time, any doubting that God in due time will strengthen you according to your need, although this may not appear at once.[52]

In the struggle to have the Scriptures do their work of strengthening the Christian's faith, carelessness must be avoided. The Christian must concentrate and fill his mind with the truth of the Bible.

> Thus I entreat you, according as necessity may remind you, to shake off your sloth and bestir yourself to do battle valiantly against Satan and the world, desiring to be dead unto yourself so as to be fully renewed in God. And because we must know before we can love, I entreat you also to exercise yourself in reading the holy exhortations that may be helps to this end. For the coldness we observe in certain persons arises from that carelessness which

---

[52]Ibid., Vol. 5, 1553, 409.

disposes them to fancy that it is enough to have relished cursorily some passage of the scriptures, without laying down as a rule to profit by it as need should require.[53]

Calvin spoke very strongly about the reality of the danger to the Christian who fails to make proper use of these means of defense. Calvin clearly taught that true faith could never be lost. Still, he could not distinguish, as a pastor, the difference between true and apparent faith in a church member. Therefore he warned those facing persecution that without proper armor they might lose their faith: "But if you do not yet feel in yourselves such an inclination, pray God that he may give it you, groaning because of your infirmity, which holds you back from doing your duty; for, as I said in the beginning, it is far too dangerous a thing to flatter our infirmities. For faith cannot be long lulled to sleep without being at last quenched."[54] The Christian must have his "sword and armour"[55] or face defeat. He must always be ready: ". . . it is necessary that a Christian, even in repose, always have one foot raised to march to battle."[56]

In the third place, while Calvin stressed the reality of the struggle and the necessity of constant battle, he also repeatedly reminded Christians that they should be assured of God's care and love. Calvin lived a life of uncompromising commitment to the Reformed faith, and he expected the same of others. For those facing persecution, exile or faithfulness in suffering were the only options. Calvin spent himself in writing to encourage the suffering and to strengthen them by reminding them of their duty. He labored to keep their faith certain.

All the exhortations which one could make to you to suffer patiently for the name of Jesus Christ and for the struggle of the

---

[53]Ibid., Vol. 6, 1554, 23.
[54]Ibid., Vol. 7, 1559, 86.
[55]Ibid., 1563, 309.
[56]*Ioannis Calvini Opera,* Brunsvigge (Schwetschke et Filium, 1873), 8, 397, from "*Quatre Sermons de M. Iehan Calvin, traictans des matieres fort utiles pour nostre temps. Le Second Sermon, contenant exhortation a souffir persecution pour suyvre Iesus Christ et son evangelie.*" An English translation of this sermon appears in Jay E. Adams, *Sermon Analysis* (Denver: Accent Books, 1986).

gospel will be pointless if we are not well assured of the cause for which we fight. Because when it is a question of leaving this life, it is indeed necessary that we be resolute and certain why it is. And such constancy can not be in us unless it is founded in the certainty of faith.[57]

The aim of the promises and exhortations of Scripture is to support and reinforce the assurance inherent in true faith. Calvin encouraged the persecuted to be assured from the Scriptures, but he also often directed their attention to God's sovereign, providential care of his own. He wrote, ". . . doubt not but God has an eye on you, and that your tears and groanings are listened to by him. For if we do not repose on his providence, the slightest distress will become an abyss to swallow us up."[58] He said, ". . . his providence . . . ought to be for us like an impregnable fortress."[59]

The power of Calvin's spiritual counsel was in the balance that he maintained between his insistence on faithfulness in the real struggles of the battle and the assurance of victory. He wrote, "Let this single consideration suffice you, that you have the assurance that God approves of your labour, when you declare a truceless war against those abominations which militate against his worship and honour."[60] The same theme sounded clearly in his sermon on suffering: "Now when I speak of such certainty I do not only mean that we know to discern between the true religion and the errors or follies of men, but also that we be well persuaded of the heavenly life and of the crown which is promised us there on high after we have fought here below."[61] Many faithful martyrs followed this advice bravely.

To the Five Prisoners of Lyons

One of the most moving episodes in Calvin's correspondence with the persecuted relates to the case of five young men who were

---

[57]Ibid., 8, 393.
[58]*Selected Works*, Vol. 6, 1557, 359ff.
[59]CO, *"Quatre Sermons,"* 8, 406.
[60]*Selected Works*, Vol. 6, 1554, 28.
[61]CO, *"Quatre Sermons,"* 8, 393ff.

imprisoned for the faith in Lyons, France in 1553. These young men had been living in Switzerland and traveled to Lyons for a visit. They were denounced to authorities as Protestants and were sent to prison where they languished for a long time.

Lyons was an important city in France, the second largest, with a population of fifty thousand. The Reformed church had been growing there slowly for several years, largely led by ministers sent from Geneva who usually preached in secret. In 1551 the Calvinists conducted a public procession through the city streets singing Psalms to demonstrate their presence in the city. The Roman Catholic authorities were distressed with good reason. (By 1562 about one-third of the city had become Reformed, and Calvinists for a few months took control of the city government.) Part of the effort to clamp down on the Protestants led to the arrest of the five young men.

Various Protestants, especially the government of Bern in Switzerland, worked diligently to obtain their release. Calvin also did what he could, but no one was able to succeed. Calvin wrote three letters to them to console and strengthen them.

A few weeks after their arrest, on June 10, 1552, Calvin writes to encourage them. He assures them that many are working to have them released. He goes on to remind them that Christians are working for them in prayer and they themselves are working in upholding the truth:

> . . . all the children of God pray for you as they are bound to do, not only on account of the mutual compassion which ought to exist between members of the same body, but because they know well that you labor for them in maintaining the cause of their salvation. . . . You see to what he has called you; doubt not, therefore, that according as he employs you, he will give you strength to fulfill his work, for he has promised this, and we know by experience that he has never failed those who allow themselves to be governed by him. Even now you have proofs of this in yourself, for he has shown his power, by giving you so much constancy in withstanding the first assaults. Be confident,

therefore, that he will not leave the work of his hand imperfect. You know what Scripture sets before us, to encourage us to fight for the cause of the Son of God; meditate upon what you have both heard and seen formerly on this head, so as to put it to practice.[62]

Calvin also writes to John Liner on August 10, 1552 to thank him for visiting the five prisoners to strengthen them. He writes:

For however despised and rejected of men, the poor believers persecuted for the sake of the Gospel may be, yet we know that God esteems them as true pearls; that there is nothing more agreeable to him than our striving to comfort and help them as much as in us lies. . . . You must also consider, that by the support which they receive from you, they are the more confirmed, for they have no doubt whatever that God has directed you to them, as indeed he has. And they have reason to lean still more firmly upon him, seeing the paternal care he shows them. Be of good courage, therefore, in this holy work, in which you serve not only God and his martyrs, but also the whole Church.[63]

Calvin writes again to the prisoners on March 7, 1553 after the appeal of their death sentence is rejected. He again compliments and encourages them: "I feel well assured that nothing shakes the firmness which he has put within you."[64] Still he recognizes the temptations and doubts that they face: "It cannot be but that you feel some twinges of frailty; yet, be confident that he whose service you are upon will so rule in your hearts by his Holy Spirit, that his grace shall overcome all temptations." Then using language almost identical to that in the Preface to his *Commentary on the Psalms*, he continues: "We who are here shall do our duty in praying that he would glorify himself more and more by your constancy, and that he may, by the consolation of his Spirit, sweeten and endear all that is bitter to the flesh, and so absorb your spirits in himself, that in contemplating that

---

[62]Calvin, *Selected Works*, Vol. 7, 351.
[63]Ibid., Vol. 7, 359, altered.
[64]Ibid., Vol. 7, 391.

heavenly crown, you may be ready without regret to leave all that belongs to this world."[65]

On May 15, 1553 just before they were to die Calvin wrote them: ". . . wherever we look here below, God has stopped the way."[66] His letters were full of consolation. He assured them that God's grace would sustain them: ". . . be confident that you shall be strengthened, according to your need, by the Spirit of our Lord Jesus, so that you shall not faint under the load of temptations, however heavy it be, any more than he did who won so glorious a victory." He reminded them of the promise of ". . . the certainty you have, that there is a heavenly life"; "being assured of the gratuitous adoption of our God, you go thither as to your inheritance."

He recognized how difficult it was to face persecution: ". . . a hard and grievous trial, to see the pride of the enemies of truth so enormous, without its getting any check from on high; their rage so unbridled, without God's interfering for the relief of his people." He urged them to confidence and prayer: "While it please God to give his enemies the rein, our duty is to be quiet, although the time of our redemption tarries." He called them to the Scriptures and to prayer. ". . . you are sufficiently careful to meditate upon what he sets before you in his word." Pray ". . . him so to subdue you to his good pleasure, that nothing may hinder you from following whithersoever he shall call."

The five prisoners died bravely and faithfully. They had learned Christian truth as taught in the Bible and ministered to them by Calvin. They embraced their bitterest afflictions, in faith dying an agonizing death, being burned alive. They went to the stake singing the Psalms. It is likely they sang Psalm 68, one of the favorite Psalms of the French Reformed:

> God shall arise, his enemies shall be scattered; and those who hate him shall flee before him! As smoke is driven away, so you shall drive them away; as wax melts before the fire, so the wicked shall perish before God! But the righteous shall be glad; they shall

[65]Ibid., Vol. 7, 392.
[66]Ibid., Vol. 7, 405–407.

exult before God; they shall be jubilant with joy! . . . Father of the fatherless and protector of widows is God in his holy habitation. God settles the solitary in a home; he leads out the prisoners to prosperity. . . .

The story of the five martyrs of Lyons was recorded in Jean Crespin's *Book of Martyrs*, first published in 1554. The stories in this important work influenced thousands, perhaps even millions, to embrace the Reformed faith. Calvin seems almost to have been a prophet about the future power of their story in his last letter to them: "Since it pleases him to employ you to the death in maintaining his quarrel, he will strengthen your hands in the fight, and will not suffer a single drop of your blood to be spent in vain. And though the fruit may not all at once appear, yet in time it shall spring up more abundantly than we can express. But as he has vouchsafed you this privilege, that your bonds have been renowned, and that the noise of them has been everywhere spread aboard, it must needs be, in despite of Satan, that your death should resound far more powerfully, so that the name of our Lord be magnified thereby."

To the Troubled Churches

In addition to his counsel to individuals, Calvin also wrote advice to churches. He wrote a particularly noteworthy letter (March 13, 1554) to a refugee church in Wezel, in the Low Countries, that was being harassed by Lutheran authorities, pressuring the Reformed church to adopt Lutheran practices. The letter shows where Calvin was willing to be flexible and where he was inflexible.

Specifically the Lutherans were insisting that the Reformed in the administration of the Lord's Supper use candles and bread that had been shaped in a particular way. Calvin writes that ideally the rite should have the "pure simplicity" taught by Christ. Properly "the moment we deviate ever so little from it, our admixture of human invention cannot fail to be a corruption." Pastors should do all they can to keep the apostolic institution and strive "to exterminate" as much as they can any "residue of Popish superstitions."[67]

Still Calvin counseled submission to the authorities. He said that the Lutheran practices were not "indifferent" and should be resisted if they were being introduced, but if they were already being used, they could be maintained. Christians should not deprive themselves of the sacrament because such ceremonies do not affect the "substance of the faith," and "it is perfectly lawful for the children of God to submit to many things of which they do not approve." ". . . we ought to make mutual concessions in all ceremonies, that do not involve any prejudice to the confession of our faith, and for this end that the unity of the church not be destroyed by our excessive rigour or moroseness." "The important consideration is that you do not yield to a faulty pliancy in the confession of your faith, and that you make no compromise as to doctrine."[68] Meanwhile the believers should make clear that they "endure rather than approve" the ceremonies.[69]

Calvin offered counsel also to churches struggling with internal dissension. Between August 1554 and December 1556 Calvin wrote several letters to try to encourage and bring peace to the French Reformed refugee church in Frankfurt. His first letter was written August 27, 1554 to a pastor of the church, Valeran Poulain, commiserating with the difficulty they faced as exiles and urging the pastor "to set them an example of modesty and moderation." It is not clear if Calvin had any information at that time that led him to believe that Poulain needed such advice, but time would show that he did.

Calvin in his November 1555 letter of condolence to Poulain's fellow pastor in Frankfurt, Richard Vauville, notes that contentions have troubled the congregation. After the death of Vauville, Calvin writes to the church (December 22, 1555), and in that letter it becomes clear that the contentions revolve around Poulain. Some are complaining that Poulain was not properly

---

[67]*Selected Works*, Vol. 6, 30.
[68]Ibid., 31.
[69]Ibid., 64.

elected as pastor and that he should resign and be reelected.[70] These scruples about the election probably reflect other points of unhappiness about his ministry. Calvin urges them not to be overly scrupulous in details of church order, especially as exiles in an environment where some Lutherans are hostile to them. He urges them to cooperate with one another and with their pastor. Then he urges them to remember their recent history and to learn to appreciate their pastor.

> Master Valeran is prepared to repel them [the hyper-Lutherans] and sustain the first attacks. That he should be molested by you into the bargain is really too extraordinary. His distress even ought to soften the hearts of those who may have had occasion to be offended with him, especially when you see that God has visited you with the plague, and that he has already taken away one of your pastors, threatening as it were to deprive you of all spiritual nourishment, since you are so little disposed to be satisfied.[71]

Calvin does not often interpret events as a specific judgment of God, and here he seems to be using all possible arguments to move the discontented in the church.

On March 3, 1556 Calvin writes again to the Frankfurt church, noting that they are still troubled. He regrets that some are "impelled by a zeal not tempered by moderation" and tells the church, ". . . it will be your duty to bring [them] to reason with all meekness and humanity." He reminds them, "For you know the rule which the Holy Spirit lays down to reconcile us with one another. It is that each should yield and give up his right, that we should seek rather to edify our neighbour in his eternal interests, than consult our own selfish desires." He also congratulates them on the new co-pastor they have called, William Olbrac. Calvin commends him and shows what he most values in a pastor: "I know him to be a man well versed in the scripture, of proper zeal

---

[70]Ibid., 241.
[71]Ibid., 243.

and straightforwardness, and so moderate and peaceable, that I should esteem him suited for this place."[72]

Again on June 24, 1556 Calvin writes to the elders and deacons of the church, concerned that troubles seem to be growing. Objections have been voiced about the regularity of the election of elders as well as the severity of discipline pressed by the elders. He urges the elders, "Especially I entreat you to preserve as much moderation as possible, not to exasperate those who are already but too much irritated."[73] In matters that are not essential Calvin clearly prizes moderation in leaders highly.

On the same day he wrote to the church as a whole, counseling every effort to advance peace:

> . . . when our hearts are embittered with animosity, suspicions must needs get the upper hand, and dispose us to put an unfavorable construction on every thing that is done by those whom we dislike, to such a pitch that from ill-will to individuals we will call white black. If things go on in this train, new evils will never cease to break out among you, and at last the mischief will acquire such intensity as to destroy everything. Wherefore we have need to bridle our affections more carefully, in order to tame and moderate them. . . . And to prove that you are desirous of a holy union with one another, let each one strive to make it up with him to whom he has been an enemy.[74]

Here Calvin shows his love of peace among God's people.

On that same day Calvin also wrote to John Clauburger, a moderate Lutheran magistrate in Frankfurt who had worked for peace in the Reformed congregation. Calvin thanks him for his help and admits the seriousness of the situation, more serious than he let on in the letters to the congregation: ". . . they are again contending with bitter hatred."[75] It is interesting that he seems to downplay the troubles in the letter to the church in order to encourage peace but is more frank with one outside the con-

---

[72]Ibid., 258.
[73]Ibid., 272.
[74]Ibid., 276ff.
[75]Ibid., 278.

gregation who might still be able to help. He also acknowledges that some of the fault is with the minister Poulain:

> . . . the pastor in question is detested by, or not very agreeable, not only to the perverse and peevish, but also to some honest and simple people, because he has not much consistency, and seldom persists in a uniform course. And though he is attacked by unjust spite, yet I know that he has lost the affections of the greater part of the church, and if they be not reconciled, a sad dispersion is at hand; nor do I see any other remedy, but that he essay to appease them, which he has promised to do, but which, as many affirm, he has not done.[76]

He recognizes that perhaps Poulain should resign for the good of the church but expresses his concern about such a course:

> I should never concede, indeed, to froward people that their pastor should yield to their perverseness, because such a thing would set a bad example, and such excessive facility would only increase the fury or audacity of his opposers. But if the greater part of the church, disgusted with their minister, can scarcely endure to listen to him, even should we grant that their disgust is unfounded, which however there is no reason to suppose, having attempted all remedies, there remains but that extreme one to which I have just now alluded.[77]

Calvin again shows a practical realism in his counsel to those who embrace sound doctrine. Sometimes for the good of the congregation ministers must go even if they are innocent.

His letter to Clauburger contains other interesting material. He offers theological reflection on whether baptism is absolutely necessary for the salvation of children. (He argues it is not.) He also defends his own ministry against some of the unfair attacks of the hyper-Lutheran ministers. Some of them had accused him of being a tyrant in theological matters. Since modern critics of

---

[76]Ibid., 279ff.
[77]Ibid., 280.

Calvin have also accused him of tyranny in Geneva, it is interesting to see his own response:

> And how vile the calumny is about my tyranny, I leave the judgment to my colleagues and brethren, who certainly have never complained that they were oppressed by my authority. Nay, they have often expostulated with me, because I am too timid. . . . I wish your ministers could see on what hard conditions I discharge my office of teaching, and that in the meantime, I arrogate nothing to myself; they would certainly, from their own good feelings, be ashamed of their rashness.[78]

In time Valeran Poulain did resign his pastoral office. On December 27, 1556 Calvin wrote to the church again. He acknowledged in this letter real problems with Poulain: "I should have thought that Master Valeran would have been somewhat more circumspect. . . . At present he confirms too clearly what has been said of him. At any rate he has shown that he is pursuing a reckless course, by which I see that God is hurrying him on to his ruin." For the congregation Calvin again urges unity: "I pray you to employ constantly every effort to unite again the body of your church which has been so miserably disperse, and for this purpose, forgetting all past quarrels and contentions, to bear with the infirmities of those who have been deceived."[79]

Calvin shows the extent of his pastoral concern in this counsel to a small church with frustrating and annoying problems. He used his energy and influence whenever he could to advance the cause of Reformed Christianity, in which he believed so passionately. His comforts and his exhortations all reflected his confidence in the Father's providential care for his people.

---

[78]Ibid., 281.
[79]Ibid., 307.

CALVIN AND THE *INSTITUTES*

John Calvin poured the fruit of his experience as a pastor and student of the Word of God into the final edition of his *Institutes of the Christian Religion*, published in 1559 in Latin. A French translation followed the next year. Calvin believed that at last this great work had both the form and the content that he had long sought.

The first edition had been published in 1536 when Calvin was only twenty-six years old. It had been intended as a brief introduction to the foundational truths of Christianity. By the Latin word *Institutio* he meant instruction in or principles of the Christian religion. That first edition had only six chapters—on the Law, on faith, on prayer, on the sacraments, on the five false sacraments of the Roman Church, and on Christian freedom and the church and the state.

Over the years Calvin added to this work in several editions, turning it into an instruction aimed more at theological students than at the church as a whole. His first revision was published in 1539, nearly tripling the length of the work. This edition was published in French in 1541. Another revision appeared in 1543 with a fourth edition published in 1550.

In the final form in 1559, much of the work continued to have positive exposition of Christian truth, but much had been added in which Calvin analyzed and critiqued the theological errors of his day. He stated the key purpose of the 1559 *Institutes*: ". . . my design in this work has been to prepare and qualify students of theology for the reading of the divine Word."[1] He believed that a clear theological system would aid the student in the study of the Bible. He was convinced that in the final edition of the *Institutes* in 1559 he had accomplished this goal to the best of his abilities: ". . . yet I never satisfied myself until it was arranged in the order in which it is now published."[2]

The final organization of the 1559 edition followed the basic order of the Apostles' Creed: Book I on the Father, Book II on the Son, Book III on the Spirit, and Book IV on the church. Yet each of these books contains much more than this bare summary would suggest.

In Book I (which comprises about 14 percent of the whole work) Calvin examines the sources of our knowledge of God (Chapters 1–10) as well as the nature of God (Chapters 11–14). He also discusses God's act of creation, especially of human beings in his image (Chapter 15), and his providential rule over his creation (Chapters 16–18).

Book II (about 19 percent of the whole) discusses first the fall of man into sin (Chapter 1), the effect of sin, especially on human beings (Chapters 2–5), and the need for Christ (Chapter 6). Then Calvin turns to the character of the Law (Chapters 7–8) and the similarities and differences of the Old and New Testaments (Chapters 9–11). Finally he examines the person of Christ (Chapters 12–14) and his saving work (Chapters 15–17).

In Book III (about 32 percent of the whole) Calvin briefly looks at the Spirit (Chapter 1) and then turns to the Spirit's great gift to the elect, namely, faith (Chapters 2–25). If B. B. Warfield, the great Princeton theologian, was right to call Calvin *the* theologian of the Holy Spirit, it is even more right to call him *the* theologian of faith. He writes of the character of faith (Chapter 2), the fruit of faith in sanctification (Chapters 3–10) and in justification (Chapters 11–19), the exercise of faith in prayer (Chapter 20), the

---

[1] John Calvin, *Institutes*, "The Author's Preface, 1559," 18.
[2] Ibid., 17, altered.

source of faith in predestination (Chapters 21–24), and finally the end of faith in the final resurrection (Chapter 25).

Book IV (about 35 percent of the whole) discusses the external means that God uses to save and preserve his people. The first means is the church, which Calvin examines in terms of its character (Chapters 1–2), its ministry and government (Chapters 3–7), and its power (Chapters 8–13). Then he turns to the sacraments as means that God uses to build up his people (Chapters 14–19) and finally looks at the state in its role as a means in the hand of God to preserve his people (Chapter 20).

Earlier chapters in this book have looked at several topics that Calvin covers in the *Institutes*, such as the church, the sacraments, the state, and faith. This chapter will follow his thought, first, on the knowledge of God derived from the Scriptures and, second, on the work of Christ to redeem his people. These two aspects of his teaching are essential to his thought and represent particularly profound and original elements of his theology.

THE SCRIPTURES

Calvin gave his life, one could say, to the Scriptures.[3] He was a student, a teacher, a preacher, and a commentator on the Bible. What did he think about the Bible, and how did his views differ from those of the medieval church?

The medieval church treasured the Bible as the very Word of God. It believed the Bible was true and invested much time and manpower in copying the Bible by hand. But the medieval church had no confidence that the Bible could be understood by those who read it. Only councils, popes, bishops, and theologians could authoritatively and reliably interpret the Bible. In reality therefore the authority in the church was not the Bible but the official teaching of the church drawn, the church believed, from the Bible and tradition. The interpretation of the Bible had become so weighed down by the accumulated traditions of the

---

[3]For a fuller discussion of aspects of Calvin on the Scriptures, see W. R. Godfrey, "Beyond the Sphere of our Judgment: Calvin and the Confirmation of Scripture," *Westminster Theological Journal*, 58 (1996), 29–39.

church that the Bible could no longer speak a genuinely reforming word to the church.

Martin Luther in the course of his studies of the Bible and theology came to recognize significant differences between what the Bible taught and what the church was teaching. He came to believe that the Bible alone must be the ultimate authority among the people of God. When he was placed on trial before the emperor at the Diet of Worms in 1521, he was asked to submit to the teaching authority of the church. He responded that he could not because "my conscience is captive to the Word of God." He believed that the Bible was not only true but was also sufficient, teaching all that Christians needed to know for salvation. He denied that the Bible needed to be supplemented with any other truth. He also taught that the Scriptures were perspicuous, by which he meant that the necessary, saving truths of the Bible were clear to its readers. He believed that the Bible could and must reform the teaching of the church.

As a young man Calvin had accepted the authority of the church's teaching. Looking back on those days, Calvin said that he had been "obstinately attached to the superstitions of the papacy." But like Luther he came to embrace the doctrine that the Bible alone was the reliable source of religious truth. Calvin rejected the medieval church's approach to the Bible where the Bible was honored, kissed, and carried in procession but was seldom opened or read by the people.

Calvin begins his *Institutes* by writing about the knowledge of God and man: "True and substantial wisdom principally consists of two parts, the knowledge of God and the knowledge of ourselves."[4] Christians need both of these kinds of knowledge, and they are interconnected. For the purpose of teaching with clarity Calvin begins his study with the question of the knowledge of God. He is not interested in abstract, philosophical reflection on God but on a practical religious knowledge of God: ". . . we are invited to a knowledge of God, not such as, content with

---

[4]Calvin, *Institutes*, I, 1, 1.

empty speculation, merely floats in the brain, but such as will be solid and fruitful, if rightly received and rooted in our hearts."[5] This true knowledge of God in its fullness will be twofold, first of God the Creator and second of God the Redeemer in Christ.[6] In these opening chapters of Book I, Calvin focuses explicitly on the knowledge of God the Creator, but what he says there applies equally to the knowledge of God the Redeemer.

The true knowledge of God is necessary for living rightly and happily: "For until men recognize that they owe everything to God, that they are supported by his paternal care, that he is the author of all the blessing they enjoy, and that nothing should be sought independently of him, they will never voluntarily submit to his authority. They will never truly and cordially devote themselves to his service, unless they rely upon him alone for true happiness."[7] This knowledge and happiness are rare: ". . . men in general render to God a formal worship, but very few truly reverence him; while great ostentation in ceremonies is universally displayed, sincerity of heart is rarely to be found."[8]

Where does this vague sense of God come from? Calvin argues that a sense of the divine is planted by God in human nature and cannot be escaped.

God has given to all some apprehension of his existence, the memory of which he frequently and insensibly renews. So as men universally know that there is a God and that he is their maker, they must be condemned by their own testimony, for not having worshipped him and consecrated their lives to his service. If we seek for ignorance of a Deity, it is most likely to be found among tribes that are the most stupid and are furthest from civilization. But, as the celebrated Cicero observes, there is no nation so barbarous, no race so savage, as not to be firmly persuaded of the being of God. Even those who in other respects appear to differ little from brutes, always retain some sense of religion.[9]

---

[5]Ibid., I, 5, 9.
[6]Ibid., I, 2, 1.
[7]Ibid., altered.
[8]Ibid., I, 2, 2, altered.
[9]Ibid., I, 3, 1, altered.

Calvin, of course, knew that some learned despisers of religion were atheists. He sounds remarkably modern.

> It is most absurd, then, to pretend, as is asserted by some, that religion was the invention of a few subtle and designing men, a political device to confine the simple multitude to their duty, while those who imposed the worship of God on others, were themselves far from believing that any god existed. I confess, indeed, that artful men have introduced many inventions into religion, to fill the vulgar with reverence, and strike them with terror, in order to obtain greater control over their minds. But this they could never have accomplished, if the minds of men had not previously possessed a firm persuasion of the existence of God, from which the propensity to religion proceeds. . . . For though there were some in ancient times, and many arise in the present age, who deny the existence of God, yet, in spite of their reluctance, they are continually receiving proofs of what they desire not to believe.[10]

Calvin continues his analysis of the knowledge of God by arguing that not only is a sense of the divine implanted in mankind, but humans also cannot evade the testimony of God found in nature: ". . . God has not only sown in the minds of men the seed of religion already mentioned, but has manifested himself in the formation of every part of the world, and daily presents himself to public view, in such a manner, that they cannot open their eyes without being forced to see him."[11]

Despite all these testimonies to God, humanity left to itself never rightly understands God. God is not at fault for this ignorance—the sinfulness of mankind is to blame. The only hope for sinners to attain a true knowledge of God is for God to reveal himself. "But whatever deficiency of natural ability prevents us from attaining the pure and clear knowledge of God, yet, since the deficiency arises from our own fault, we are left without any excuse."[12] The only solution to this problem is that God must

[10]Ibid., I, 3, 2, altered.
[11]Ibid., I, 5, 1, altered.
[12]Ibid., I, 5, 15.

reveal himself to us in words we can know and understand. Despite the revelation of God that surrounds us,

> . . . we need another and better assistance. . . . So he has not unnecessarily added the light of his Word, to make himself known unto salvation, and has honored with this privilege those whom he intended to unite in a more close and familiar connection with himself. . . . For, as persons who are old, or whose eyes are by any means become dim, if you show them the most beautiful book, though they perceive something written, they can scarcely read two words together. But with the assistance of spectacles they will begin to read distinctly. Just so Scripture, collecting in our minds the otherwise confused notions of Deity, dispels the darkness, and gives us a clear view of the true God. This, then, is a singular favor, that, in the instruction of the church, God not only uses mute teachers but even opens his own sacred mouth.[13]

In history the revelation of God was given by various visions and prophecies, but to ensure that all generations of God's people might have his Word, God caused his truth to be written down and preserved in the Bible.

> But, whether God revealed himself to the patriarchs by oracles and visions, or suggested, by means of the ministry of men, what should be handed down by tradition to their posterity, it is beyond a doubt that their minds were impressed with a firm assurance of the doctrine, so that they were persuaded and convinced that the information they had received came from God. For God always secured to his Word an undoubted credit, superior to all human opinion. At length, that truth might remain in the world in a continual course of instruction to all ages, he determined that the same oracles which he had deposited with the patriarchs should be committed to public record.[14]

This inscripturated revelation that is the Bible is absolutely necessary for the people of God: "For, since the human mind is

---

[13]Ibid., I, 6, 1, altered.
[14]Ibid., I, 6, 2, altered.

unable, through its stupidity, to attain any knowledge of God without the assistance of his sacred Word, all mankind, except for the Jews, as they sought God without the Word, must necessarily have been wandering in vanity and error."[15]

In order for us to know God, God must reveal himself. Left to themselves, people will know only the false truths they invent for themselves. "For, if we consider the mutability of the human mind, how easy its fall into forgetfulness of God; how great its propensity to errors of every kind; how violent its rage for the perpetual fashioning of new and false religions, it will be easy to perceive the necessity of heavenly doctrine being committed to writing, that it might not be lost in oblivion, or evaporate in error, or be corrupted by the presumption of men."[16] As Calvin had written early in his ministry to Cardinal Sadoleto, "A soul, therefore, when deprived of the Word of God, is given up unarmed to the devil for destruction."[17]

Since God has given the knowledge of himself in the Bible, Christians must recognize how truly and fully they learn the truth about him there. The Bible is entirely true and trustworthy. Christians know the truthfulness by recognizing that God is the ultimate author of the Bible: ". . . the Scriptures obtain the same complete credit and authority with believers, when they are satisfied of its divine origin, as if they heard the very words pronounced by God himself."[18] Since God is the source of the Bible, the church can be sure that the truth revealed there is one consistent truth throughout: "He is the author of the Scriptures: he cannot be changeable and inconsistent with himself."[19]

As the Scriptures that come from God are absolutely true and reliable, they can be trusted absolutely. The truth of the Word is impressed on the people of God by his Spirit: "For the Lord has established a kind of mutual connection between

[15]Ibid., I, 6, 4, altered.
[16]Ibid., I, 6, 3, altered.
[17]John Calvin, "Reply to Sadoleto," *Selected Works of John Calvin*, Vol. 1, ed. H. Beveridge and J. Bonnet (Grand Rapids, MI: Baker, 1983), 53.
[18]Calvin, *Institutes*, I, 7, 1, altered.
[19]Ibid., I, 9, 2, altered.

the certainty of his Word and of his Spirit; so that our minds are filled with a solid reverence for the Word, when by the light of the Spirit we are enabled to behold in it God's face; and, on the other hand, without the least fear of mistake, we gladly receive the Spirit, when we recognize him in his image, that is, in the Word."[20]

Precisely because the Word is so true and so necessary, Calvin throughout his career stressed the duty of the whole church and of each of God's people to honor and follow that Word alone. Early in his career he had written to Sadoleto: ". . . ours the Church whose supreme care it is humbly and religiously to venerate the Word of God, and submit to its authority."[21] Similarly in his commentary on the Psalms he sees acceptance of the Bible as a key evidence of fidelity to God: "Their contempt of God he proves from their want of reverential deference to his Word; subjection to the Word of God, and cordial submission to his precepts and instructions, being the surest test of religious principle."[22] The Bible must be the beloved and honored authority for the whole life of the church.

For Calvin the doctrine of Scripture is not just one doctrine among many but is rather a central link in a chain that includes faith, hope, assurance, the work of the Spirit, and eternal life. He eloquently expressed that interrelationship:

> This indeed is the chief point of faith, That the word of God is not only distinguished for fidelity and steadfastness for a time, but that it continues unchangeable for ever. Were it otherwise, it could not include within it the hope of eternal salvation. That the assurance of this immutability of God's word may be rooted in our minds, the inward revelation of the Holy Spirit is indeed necessary; for until God seal within us the certainty of his word, our belief of its certainty will be continually wavering. Yet the Prophet, not without cause, affirms, that he learned this truth from the word; for when God shines into us by his Spirit, he at

---

[20]Ibid., I, 9, 3, altered.
[21]Calvin, "Reply to Sadoleto," 50.
[22]Calvin, *Commentary on Psalms*, Vol. 2, on Ps. 50:17, 276.

the same time causes that sacred truth which endures for ever to shine forth in the mirror of his word.[23]

The truthfulness and reliability of the Word is foundational for Calvin, but it is by no means the whole doctrine of Scripture. Calvin insisted that the Bible is also sufficient to guide the church into all truth and Christian living. The medieval church had come to supplement the Bible with many practices and traditions that it claimed were ancient and apostolic. Calvin argued that not only did such traditions detract from and often contradict biblical religion, but they laid an unbearable burden on the people of God. The church to be the true church of God should recognize that everything God's people need for true religion is to be found in the Bible.

> For this reason we freely censure that tyranny of human traditions, which is imposed upon the world in the name of the church. Nor do we hold the church in contempt, as our adversaries falsely assert, in order to make us hated. . . . They are themselves the most outrageous violators of the church . . . in their combination of impudence and wickedness shown in their incessant clamoring about the authority of the church, while they take no notice of the command of the Lord, or of the obedience due from the church to that command.[24]

Calvin throughout the *Institutes* examines and rejects many abuses of the Roman Church in imposing human traditions on Christian consciences. His rejection of human traditions is not limited to Rome, however, but applies to all human additions to the Word of God. Calvin then argues that human traditions are to be rejected whatever the time or circumstances: ". . . as to the human traditions of all ages, which ought to be rejected and repudiated by the church and all pious persons, the direction we have already given is clear and certain—that they are all laws made by men without the Word of God, for the purpose, either of

---

[23]Ibid., Vol. 3, on Ps. 119:152, 29.
[24]Calvin, *Institutes*, IV, 10, 18, altered.

prescribing any method for the worship of God, or of laying the conscience under a religious obligation, as if they imposed things necessary for salvation."[25]

This rejection of the authority of tradition had guided him from the beginning of his ministry. It is embedded in the early confession of the church in Geneva: ". . . we affirm that we desire to follow Scripture alone as rule of faith and religion . . . without addition or diminution."[26]

For Calvin, then, the Bible is true and sufficient. But a third conviction is critical to the understanding of the Bible. The Scriptures are clear and understandable in teaching the saving message of God. This doctrine of the perspicuity of Scripture does not assert that every verse of the Bible is crystal-clear to every reader, but rather that the great truth of salvation is clear to the careful reader of the Bible as a whole.

In contrast to this doctrine, Rome had argued that while the Bible certainly is the true Word of God, it is a difficult book to interpret and that therefore the Lord had established in the church authoritative interpreters of the Bible, namely, the Pope aided by his bishops and doctors. Only these interpreters could provide the church with a certain and reliable understanding.

Calvin rejected such an idea for several reasons. First, the Bible itself does not establish such an office of infallible interpreters of the Word. Second, and more importantly, the claim for the need of such interpreters is an insult to God and to the Scriptures. Surely God in revealing himself could and would reveal himself successfully. The Bible testifies that God did in fact reveal himself clearly. Calvin taught:

> It is true, that the law and the gospel contain mysteries which far transcend our capacities. But since God illumines the minds of his people with the spirit of understanding, to grasp these mysteries which he has condescended to reveal in his Word, there we have

---

[25]Ibid., IV, 10, 16, altered.
[26]*John Calvin: Theological Treatises*, "Confession of Faith, 1536," Article 1, ed. J.K.S. Reid (Philadelphia: Westminster, 1954), 260.

now no abyss, but a way in which we may safely walk, and a lamp for the direction of our feet, the light of life, and the school of certain and evident truth.[27]

In his commentaries he returns again and again to the importance of the clarity of the Word: "Were there such obscurity in God's word, as the Papists foolishly talk about, the commendation with which the prophet here honours the law would be altogether undeserved. Let us, then, be assured that an unerring light is to be found there, provided we open our eyes to behold it."[28]

Calvin recognizes that not everything in the Bible is immediately clear to everyone. But he insists that the Bible is clear enough "to meet our needs." In commenting on the biblical text about seeing in a mirror dimly, he wrote:

> . . . the knowledge of God, which we now have from his word, is indeed certain and true, and has nothing in it that is confused, or perplexed, or dark, but is spoken of as comparatively obscure, because it comes far short of that clear manifestation to which we look forward; for then we shall see face to face. Thus this passage is not at all at variance with other passages, which speak of the clearness, at one time, of the law, at another time, of the entire Scripture, but more especially of the gospel. For we have in the word (in so far as is expedient for us) a naked and open revelation of God, and it has nothing intricate in it, to hold us in suspense, as wicked persons imagine.[29]

Calvin was not naive about this doctrine and certainly recognized that Christians would at times come to differing interpretations of the Bible. He insists, however, that the source of such differences is in the readers, not in the Word: "This enables us to see clearly how wicked are the speeches of those who say that no certainty can be obtained from the word, and who pretend

---

[27]Calvin, *Institutes*, I, 17, 2, altered.
[28]John Calvin, *Commentary on Psalms*, Vol. 4, on Ps. 119:105, 480.
[29]John Calvin, *Commentary on I Corinthians* (Grand Rapids, MI: Baker, 1979), on 13:12, 430–431.

that it is a nose of wax, in order to deter others from reading it; for thus do wicked men blaspheme, because the mere doctrine of the word exposes and refutes their errors. But we reply with David, 'Thy word, O Lord, is a lamp to our feet, and a light to our paths.' (Psalm cxix. 105.) We reply with Isaiah and the rest of the prophets, that the Lord has taught nothing that is obscure, or ambiguous, or false."[30] When Christians differ, the only path to resolving differences is by more careful and faithful study of the Bible.

Calvin throughout his writing is emphatic about the Bible— its necessity, its divine origin, its absolute truthfulness, its sufficiency, and its clarity. He goes even further in his doctrine of Scripture, asking a critical question: How does someone know that the Scriptures are the revelation of God?

Calvin addressed this question in the *Institutes*, Book I, Chapters 7–8. In these chapters he rejects two possible answers to this question. A first possible answer was that one knows the authority of the Bible from the teaching authority of the church. Calvin, however, rejected this answer, insisting that the church rested on the Bible, not the Bible on the church. God's revelation creates and gathers the church, the people of God.

A second possible answer was that one comes to know the authority of the Bible by human, rational evaluation. Calvin, particularly in Chapter 8 of Book I, did examine the appropriate ways in which various kinds of evidence could be used by human reason to substantiate the truthfulness and authority of the Bible.[31] He believed that the evidence available to the human mind was indeed more than adequate to convince any thoughtful person that the Bible is the Word of God. The evidence to which

---

[30]John Calvin, *Commentary on Isaiah*, Vol. 3 (Grand Rapids, MI: Baker, 1979), on 45:19.

[31]T. H. L. Parker, *Calvin's Doctrine of the Knowledge of God* (Edinburgh: Oliver and Boyd, 1969), 74, from a neoorthodox perspective, seems to like the way in which Calvin approaches the confirmation of Scripture in *Institutes*, I, 7 but is very disparaging about his use of evidences in Chapter 8: "Some are certainly more weighty than others; but strong or weak they collectively constitute a blemish on Calvin's doctrine of the Word of God which has had for its progeny the busyness of fundamentalists to prove the truth of the Bible to the neglect of discovering and preaching the Truth of the Bible."

he points includes the agreement of the various parts of the Bible with one another, the great antiquity of the texts, the miracles that accompanied the revelation, the prophecies fulfilled, the divine preservation of the Bible over centuries, and the testimony of the whole church in all ages, especially the testimony of the martyrs. He made clear, however, that the use of evidence is a secondary and supportive element for knowing the Scriptures' authority. The primary and ultimately foundational way to know the authority of Scripture is to be found elsewhere.

For Calvin, if the authority of Scripture rests on the church or on rational proofs, then it rests on a human authority. But he believed such a position was disastrous for true religion. ". . . what will be the condition of those wretched consciences, which are seeking a solid assurance of eternal life, if all the promises which we have concerning it rest only on the judgment of men?"[32] For Calvin, man must have a certain and undoubted foundation for religious knowledge. The Bible is that foundation, and its truth must be known by some manner other than human judgment. As Calvin said in his "Reply to Sadoleto," "We hold that the Word of God alone lies beyond the sphere of our judgment."[33]

Still the question remains: How can people know without exercising their judgment? Calvin's answer is that the Holy Spirit convinces God's people of the truth of his Word:

> . . . the testimony of the Spirit is superior to all reason. For as God alone is a sufficient witness of himself in his Word, so also the Word will never gain credit in the hearts of men, till it be confirmed by the internal testimony of the Spirit. It is necessary, therefore, that the same Spirit, who has spoken by the mouths of the prophets, should penetrate into our hearts, to convince us that they faithfully delivered the oracles which were entrusted to them by God. . . . Some good men are troubled that they are not always prepared with clear proof to oppose the impious, when they murmur with impunity against God's Word; as though the

---

[32]Calvin, *Institutes*, I,7,1, altered.
[33]Calvin, "Reply to Sadoleto," 66.

Spirit were not for this reason called a "seal" and a "guarantee," for confirming the faith of the pious; because until he illumines their minds, they are perpetually fluctuating among a multitude of doubts.[34]

This work of the Spirit transcends the human reasoning process and establishes Scripture above every human authority. The real self-authenticating character of the Bible is found in the work of the Spirit, who first inspired it and then applies it to the believer. Again Calvin states:

> For though the Scripture wins our reverence by its internal majesty, it never seriously affects us until it is confirmed by the Spirit in our hearts. Therefore, being illumined by him, we now believe the divine original of the Scripture, not from our own judgment or that of others, but we value the certainty, that we have received it from God's own mouth by the ministry of men, to be superior to that of any human judgment, and equal to an intuitive perception of God himself in it. We seek no arguments or probabilities to support our judgment, but submit our judgments and understandings as to a thing concerning which it is impossible for us to judge.[35]

How did the Spirit work that certainty in the believer? Calvin describes that work in rather metaphorical language. His description is brief and far from any full philosophical analysis. His primary metaphor is that of illumination—a light that enlightens the blind. "The Word of God is like the sun, shining on all to whom it is preached; but without any benefit to the blind. But since we are all blind by nature, it cannot penetrate into our minds, unless the internal teacher, the Spirit, make way for it by his illumination."[36] He also speaks of it as a taste: "How shall we learn to distinguish light from darkness, white from black, sweet from bitter? For Scripture exhibits as clear evidence of its truth, as white and black things do of their color, or sweet and bitter things

---

[34]Calvin, *Institutes*, 1.7.4, altered.
[35]Ibid., I,7,5, altered.
[36]Ibid., III, 2, 34.

do of their taste."[37] This light or feeling or taste is a profound, immediate experience worked in the believer by the Spirit.

Calvin argues that by the power of the Spirit one can gain a higher understanding and a deeper insight into truth. Again Calvin's language was more rhetorical than technically philosophical. "For faith is so superior, that the human mind must exceed and rise above itself, in order to attain it. Nor does the mind which attains it comprehend what it perceives, but being persuaded of that which it cannot comprehend, it understands more by the certainty of this persuasion, than it would comprehend of any human object by the exercise of its natural capacity."[38] And in another place Calvin writes:

> Therefore, as we can never come to Christ unless we are drawn by the Spirit of God, so when we are drawn, we are raised both in mind and in heart above the reach of our understanding. For illumined by him, the soul received, as it were, new eyes for the contemplation of the heavenly mysteries, whose splendor had previously dazzled it. And thus the human intellect, irradiated by the light of the Holy Spirit, then begins to relish those things which pertain to the kingdom of God, for which before it had not the smallest taste.[39]

Some have argued that Calvin's view of the Spirit's confirmation of the Scripture is mystical and irrational. Such a reading of Calvin seriously misunderstands him. For Calvin the human mind can rationally see the authority of the Bible, but the human mind is not the certain foundation that Christian faith needs. That foundation is found in the unique work of the Spirit convincing the elect of the Bible's truth.

In summary, the key elements in Calvin's view of the primary confirmation of Scripture are these: (1) Christians know the Scriptures to be the Word of God by an immediate recognition of that truth. (It is important to bear in mind here that

---

[37]Ibid., I, 7, 2, altered.
[38]Ibid., III, 2, 14, altered.
[39]Ibid., III, 2, 34.

Calvin is speaking of the theological foundation of Christian confidence in the Bible as the Word of God, not the process by which a Christian in his own experience may come to that confidence.) (2) This knowledge is a unique response to the Word of God. (3) This knowledge is worked by the Holy Spirit. (4) The Holy Spirit works this knowledge in the renewed minds and hearts of Christians. (5) This knowledge is foundational to religious certainty and confidence. And (6) this knowledge is supported and reinforced by the evidence available to human reason.

Calvin stresses the significance of his position on the confirmation of Scripture passionately for a variety of reasons. The first is the importance of religious certainty. At the heart of Calvin's understanding of the gospel is the conviction that the promises of God must be certain and apprehended by a confident faith. He sees faith as a deep trust in God's fatherly goodness:

> For, as faith is not content with a dubious and changeable opinion, so is it neither content with an obscure and perplexed conception; but requires a full and fixed certainty, such as is commonly acquired about matters that have been tested and proved. For unbelief is so deeply rooted in our hearts, and such is our propensity to it, that though all men confess with the tongue, that God is faithful, no man can persuade himself of the truth of it, without the most strenuous efforts. Especially when the time of trial comes, each one's wavering uncovers the fault previously concealed. Nor is it without reason that the Holy Spirit asserts the authority of the Word of God with such high praise, designing to remedy the disease that I have mentioned, that the promises of God may obtain full credit with us.[40]

At the heart of the gospel is the truth and certainty of Christ as Savior, taught to man by the Spirit through the Word.

Calvin also stresses the work of the Spirit in knowing the Bible's authority for polemic and apologetic reasons. The greatest opponent that Calvin faced was the Roman Catholic Church of his day. Rome insisted that the authority of the Bible rested on

---

[40]Ibid., III, 2, 15, altered.

the authority of an infallible church. This disagreement over the ultimate authority for Christians was one issue at the heart of the Reformation. Rome argued that the canon, text, authority, and interpretation of the Bible all rested on the recognition and interpretation given them by the teaching authority of the church. The Reformers, in response, argued for the authority of the Bible as establishing the church and standing over the church to reform it. For Calvin the work of the Spirit replaces the role that Rome gives to the church as the ultimate authority confirming the Scriptures as God's Word.

Equally Calvin rejects any human claim to new revelations by the Spirit in his day apart from the Word. Calvin utterly dismisses the claims of certain fanatics in his day that they received revelations from the Spirit beyond what was taught in the Bible. Individual judgment, even in the name of the Holy Spirit, could no more stand over the Word than could the corporate judgment of the church.

Calvin clearly teaches that the Bible is the true and certain Word of God. But some scholars suggest that his actual statements on the Bible in his commentaries show that he does not treat all the words of the Bible as true and of divine origin. They argue that Calvin's doctrine of Scripture that he presents in the *Institutes* is quite different from the way he actually examines and explains the text of the Bible in his commentaries. Such a contradiction between Calvin the theologian and Calvin the commentator, of course, seems inherently unlikely. Surely Calvin would have noticed such a problem.

Still at first glance these scholars seem to have a case. In his commentaries Calvin does rather frequently say things like "the expression is not strictly accurate" or "Paul would have been more correct." But in context it is clear that Calvin is never suggesting that the human authors of the Bible have made a mistake or introduced an error into the text. Calvin's apparently critical statements are actually part of Calvin's understanding of the language of Scripture as accommodated to the needs of the readers or of his rhetorical analysis of the language of the text in terms of ancient literary standards of eloquence. In context, on the first quotation above, Calvin is explaining a text in this way: "When Christ says, that 'the priests *profane* the Sabbath,' the expression is not strictly accurate, and is accommodated to his hearers."[41] On the second quotation in context, Calvin wrote, "Paul would have been more correct if he had contrasted the rising of the Gentiles with the fall of the Jews. I make this point to prevent anyone from looking here for ornate language, or taking offense at this bluntness of speech. Paul's writings were not intended to turn the tongue to eloquence but to mould the heart."[42] The Bible is always true even if not always elegant by Ciceronian standards.

In fact, Calvin goes out of his way in his commentaries again and again to articulate the high doctrine of Scripture that he teaches in his *Institutes*. For example, on the harmony of the accounts in the four Gospels, he writes, "Indeed God's Spirit, who appointed the Evangelists as recorders, deliberately controlled their pen, so that all should write in complete agreement, but in different ways. It gave more certainty and light to God's truth when it was established that His witnesses did not tell a pre-arranged tale, but each of them, without respect to the other, wrote simply and freely what the Spirit dictated."[43]

Calvin also defends the accuracy and truthfulness of paraphrased quotations from the Old Testament in the New Testament: "We must always observe the rule, that as often as the Apostles quote a testimony from Scripture, although they do not render it word for word, in fact may move quite a way from it, they adapt it suitably and appropriately to the case in hand. So readers should always take care to note the object of the passages of Scripture that the Evangelists use, not to press single words too exactly, but to be content with the one message which they never

[41]John Calvin, *Commentary on a Harmony of the Evangelists, Matthew, Mark, and Luke*, Vol. 2, trans. W. A. Morrison (Grand Rapids, MI: Baker, 1979), on Matt. 12:5, 49.

[42]John Calvin, *Commentary on Romans* (Grand Rapids, MI: Eerdmans, 1976), on 11:12, 247.

[43]John Calvin, *Commentary on the Harmony of the Gospels* (Grand Rapids, MI: Eerdmans, 1972), on Matt. 2:1, 82.

take from Scripture to distort into a foreign sense, but suit correctly to its real purpose."[44]

For Calvin the reliability of the Bible in every way is necessary for the spiritual well-being of Christians. "Whoever, therefore, would desire to persevere in uprightness and integrity of life, let them learn to exercise themselves daily in the study of the word of God; for, whenever a man despises or neglects instruction, he easily falls into carelessness and stupidity, and all fear of God vanishes from his mind."[45] Calvin's stress upon this point translated into a religious heritage among the Reformed where church members became deeply imbued with a knowledge of the Bible and sought in it spiritual direction and strength.

All of Calvin's carefully developed doctrine of Scripture has one great goal: that the people of God might know with certainty the salvation God has provided for his people in Christ. While he is often very eloquent and sophisticated about this in his commentaries and in his *Institutes*, he is also very simple and forceful about it in his Genevan Catechism. The following questions and answers show how closely Calvin linked his doctrine of Scripture with his doctrine of salvation in the work of Christ.

> M [Minister]: Where will this [God's love] be apparent to us?
> C [Catechist]: In his Word, where he reveals his mercy to us in Christ, and testifies of his love towards us.
> M: Then the foundation and beginning of faith in God is to know him in Christ? (John 17:3).
> C: Quite so.[46]

> M: What are we to conclude from the matters that have been treated by us?
> C: What truth itself teaches and I proposed at the beginning: this is life eternal, to know the one true God as Father and Jesus Christ whom he sent (John 17:3). I say to know him, in order that we may offer to him the honour and worship that is due,

---

[44]Ibid., on Matt. 2:6, 85ff.
[45]Calvin, *Commentary on Psalms*, Vol. 1, on Ps. 18:22, 283.
[46]Calvin, "Genevan Catechism," Q. 13–14, 92.

so that he be not only Lord to us, but also Father and Saviour (Matt. 1:21), that we on our side be his children and servants, and accordingly dedicate our life to display his glory.

M: By what road does one come to such blessedness?

C: To this end God has left us his sacred Word. For spiritual doctrine is a kind of door, by which we enter into his celestial Kingdom.[47]

M: Where must we seek this Word?

C: In the Holy Scriptures in which it is contained.

M: How should it be used to obtain profit from it?

C: If we lay hold on it with complete heartfelt conviction as nothing less than certain truth come down from heaven; if we show ourselves docile to it; if we subdue our wills and minds to his obedience; if we love it heartily; if having it once engraved on our hearts and its roots fixed there so that it bring forth fruit in our life; if finally we be formed to its rule—then it will turn to our salvation, as intended. . . .

M: But are we not to apply diligence and strive with all zeal to advance in it by reading, hearing and meditating?

C: Certainly; while everyone ought to exercise himself in daily reading, at the same time also all are to attend with special regularity the gatherings where the doctrine of salvation is expounded in the company of the faithful.[48]

In all his work Calvin urges Christians to grow in grace by growing in their knowledge of the Bible: "So far, then, as each of us shall desire to make progress in the knowledge of Christ, it will be necessary that Scripture shall be the subject of our diligent and constant meditation."[49]

THE WORK OF CHRIST

Calvin shows the ultimate purpose of Scripture in his discussion of the work of Christ in his 1559 *Institutes*. The Scriptures make God known, especially God in Christ as the redeemer of sinners.

---

[47]Ibid., Q. 300–301, 129.
[48]Ibid., Q. 302–303, 305, 130.
[49]John Calvin, *Commentary on the Gospel according to John*, trans. W. Pringle (Grand Rapids, MI: Baker, 1979), on 2:17, 95.

Calvin's reflections on the work of Christ are relatively brief because in a sense the doctrine of the work of Christ was not a controversial issue in the sixteenth century. Roman Catholics as well as the Reformers believed that salvation flowed from the work of Christ. The debate between Protestants and Roman Catholics was about how the work of Christ was received (specifically by faith—the theme of Book III—and through the ministry of the church—the theme of Book IV). Still the writing of Calvin on the work of Christ has remarkable insights.

Calvin makes clear that Christ is the pivotal point for all Christian knowledge and life. Christ is the center of the Bible and the Christian message. He shows that clearly in the brief but critical Chapter 6 of Book II. After writing about three hundred pages on the knowledge of God, Calvin writes in this little chapter, "Therefore, since we have fallen from life into death, all that knowledge of God as the Creator that we have discussed would be useless unless it were succeeded by faith exhibiting God to us as Father in Christ."[50]

Christians can only know God by knowing him in Christ. Nature and reason can never teach sinners that God is their Father. "For though God is pleased still to manifest his fatherly kindness to us in various ways, yet we cannot by contemplating the world conclude that he is our Father."[51] Only through Christ can anyone know that God is Father. This knowledge was given to Old Testament believers as well to New Testament believers. "Christ was always set before the holy fathers under the law, as the object to which they should direct their faith."[52]

The love of God and the assurance of salvation are to be found only in Christ: ". . . unless God reveal himself to us in Christ, we cannot have that knowledge of him which is necessary to salvation. . . . God is apprehended [as Father] in Christ, and in him alone."[53] As Christ is at the center of Christian faith, so his work is the foundation of salvation.

---

[50]Calvin, *Institutes*, II, 6, 1, altered.
[51]Ibid., altered.
[52]Ibid., II, 6, 2, altered.
[53]Ibid., II, 6, 4, altered.

For the first time in the history of the church Calvin develops an understanding of the work of Christ in terms of Christ's offices of prophet, priest, and king. Calvin's great mentor and friend Martin Bucer may first have suggested these three offices as a way of understanding Christ, but Calvin was the first to develop them. "Therefore, that faith may find in Christ a solid ground of salvation, and may rely on him, it is proper for us to establish this principle, that the office which was assigned to him by the Father consists of three parts. For he was given as a prophet, a king, and a priest."[54]

Christ is the great and final prophet who brings the true and complete doctrine of God and of salvation. "Now it is to be observed that the title 'Christ' belongs to these three offices. For we know that under the law not only priests and kings, but prophets also were anointed with holy oil." Christ ". . . received this anointing, not only for himself that he might carry out the office of a teacher, but for his whole body, that the preaching of the gospel might continually be attended with the power of the Spirit. But it remains beyond all doubt, that by this perfection of doctrine which he has introduced, he has put an end to all prophecies. Those who, not contented with the gospel, make any extraneous addition to it, are guilty of detracting from his authority."[55] As prophet Christ works to teach the full and final revelation of God for the salvation of his people.

Calvin stresses that as the true King, Christ rules over and protects his people. "There is no doubt that God here promises to be the everlasting governor and defender of his church. . . . Amid the turbulent agitations with which it [the true church] is incessantly harassed, and amid the painful and formidable commotions which menace it with innumerable calamities, it may still be preserved in safety."[56] Christ as the present King of his people constantly protects and defends them for their good and his glory.

---

[54]Ibid., II, 15, 1, altered.
[55]Ibid., II, 15, 2, altered.
[56]Ibid., II, 15, 3, altered.

Christ as present King also blesses his people with the gift of the Spirit. "For the Holy Spirit has chosen Christ as his residence, that those heavenly riches, which we so greatly need, may be copiously distributed to us from him. Now the faithful stand invincible in the strength of their king and are enriched with his spiritual blessings."[57] The Spirit equips the people of God with all that they need to serve Christ.

Christ is not only the present King of his people, but he is also their future eternal King. "What advantage, then, could come to us from being gathered under the government of the heavenly king, if the benefit of it were not to extend beyond the present life? It ought therefore to be known, that whatever happiness is promised us in Christ, consists not in external success, such as a life of joy and tranquility, abundant wealth, security from every injury, and numerous delights suited to our carnal desires, but that it is peculiar to the heavenly life."[58] Christ the King guarantees future heavenly blessedness.

As the true priest, Christ pays for the sins of his people by the sacrifice of his own body. "The priestly dignity belongs exclusively to Christ because by the sacrifice of his death, he has abolished our guilt and made satisfaction for our sins . . . a new and different method has been adopted in the case of Christ, that the sacrifice should also be the priest." And as priest Christ makes all of his people into priests under him. "For we who are polluted in ourselves, being 'made priests' in him, offer ourselves and all our services to God, and enter boldly into the heavenly sanctuary, so that the sacrifices of prayers and praise which proceed for us, are 'acceptable' and 'a sweet-smelling savor' in the presence of God."[59]

Calvin does not develop in his discussion of Christ's priesthood or kingship what later Reformed theology would call the active obedience of Christ. The doctrine of the active obedience teaches that Christ perfectly kept the Law in the place of and for

---

[57]Ibid., II, 15, 5, altered.
[58]Ibid., II, 15, 4, altered.
[59]Ibid., II, 15, 6, altered.

the sake of his people. But he clearly teaches this doctrine else-where. For example, in writing of Christ as mediator, Calvin sees him as the second Adam who obeyed for his people: "Our Lord then made his appearance as a real man. He put on the character of Adam, and assumed his name, to act as his substitute in his obedience to the Father, to lay down our flesh as the price of satisfaction to the justice of God, and to suffer the punishment which we had deserved, in the same nature in which the offence had been committed."[60]

At another place Calvin underscores the importance of Christ's active obedience in his redemptive work:

> Now, in answer to the inquiry, how Christ, by the abolition of our sins, has destroyed the enmity between God and us, and procured a righteousness to render him favorable and propitious to us, it may be replied in general, that he accomplished it for us by the whole course of his obedience. . . . Paul extends the cause of the pardon which exempts us from the curse of the law, to the whole life of Christ. . . . Thus he himself affirmed even in his baptism to be a branch of his righteousness, because he acted in obedience to the command of the Father. In short, from the time of his assuming the character of a servant, he began to pay the price of our deliverance in order to redeem us.[61]

In particular Calvin makes clear that Christ's active obe-dience is foundational to his thought on justification as the righteousness that is imputed to his people: "Thus we simply explain justification to be an acceptance, by which God receives us into his favor, and esteems us as righteous persons. And we say that it consists in the remission of sins and the imputation of the righteousness of Christ."[62] Christ was indeed obedient in the place of his people as a critical part of their justification: "Now, we describe this righteousness in the following manner: That a sinner, being admitted to communion with Christ, is by

[60]Ibid., II, 12, 3, altered.
[61]Ibid., II, 16, 5, altered.
[62]Ibid., III, 11, 2, altered.

his grace reconciled to God; while, being purified by his blood, he obtains remission of sins, and being clothed in his righteousness, as if it were his own, he stands secure before the heavenly tribunal."[63] Calvin certainly teaches active obedience clearly even if he does not integrate it into his discussions of the three offices of Christ.

Calvin eloquently summarizes how all of salvation is to be found in Christ and in him alone:

> Since we see that the whole of our salvation, and all the branches of it, are comprehended in Christ, we must be cautious not to separate him from the smallest portion of it. If we seek salvation, we are taught by the name of Jesus, that it is in him; if we seek any other gifts of the Spirit, they will be found in his anointing; strength, in his dominion; purity, in his conception; gentleness discovers itself in his nativity, by which he was made to resemble us in all things, that he might learn to commiserate with us. If we seek redemption, it will be found in his passion; if absolution, in his condemnation; remission of the curse, in his cross; satisfaction, in his sacrifice; purification, in his blood; reconciliation, in his descent into hell; mortification of the flesh, in his tomb; newness of life and immortality, in his resurrection; the inheritance of the celestial kingdom, in his entrance into heaven; protection, security, abundance, and enjoyment of all blessings, in his kingdom; a fearless expectation of the judgment, in the judicial authority committed to him. Finally, blessings of every kind are deposited in him; let us draw from his treasury, and from no other source, until our desires are satisfied.[64]

Calvin's *Institutes of the Christian Religion* is undoubtedly a great work of theology and a demonstration that Calvin is one of the great theologians in the history of the church. But even more the *Institutes* demonstrate that Calvin is always the pastor stressing the essential elements of true religion. The knowledge of God and the work of Christ are foundational to all that he preached and taught.

---

[63]Ibid., III, 17, 8.
[64]Ibid., II, 16, 19, altered.

CONCLUSION: THE UNMARKED GRAVE

Calvin's health was never very good in the latter part of his life. His overwork had certainly contributed to his physical decline. He died at age fifty-four, worn-out. Yet he had worked with great energy, faithfulness, and productivity throughout his life. He had written commentaries on all the books of the New Testament except 2 and 3 John and the book of Revelation. He had published commentaries or lectures on many of the Old Testament books. He had written many theological treatises and volumes of correspondence in addition to all of the sermons he had preached.

Much of his work had been done in great haste and under great pressure. For example, late in his life he expressed regret that he had not had time to revise the Genevan Catechism that he had written on his return from Strassburg. The city council had promised to encourage people to learn this catechism. So Calvin wrote it quickly, fearing that the council would change its mind and he would miss a great opportunity. In fact, when he finished writing a question or two, someone would rush the text to the printer to be typeset. Calvin had no chance to review or revise what he had written and no opportunity to get advice from others. He wished he could have taken more time in preparing it. But Calvin was an active pastor, not a leisurely academic in all that he wrote.

For much of his life he slept relatively little and ate little. As early as his days in Strassburg, the strain of his life was beginning to tell. By 1559 his health problems were becoming great—

regular bouts of malaria-like fever, tuberculosis, ulcerated veins, kidney stones, and hemorrhoids. His letters, usually reflecting little of his personal life, did express something of his physical suffering.

Out of his own sufferings and the sufferings of the people of God that he observed as a pastor he often thought about the contradictions of the Christian's life. He identified with the people of God because he wrestled with the same problems that they faced—sin, sickness, persecution, exile, hatred, divisions in family and church.

He gave poignant expression to that suffering in his commentary on Hebrews 11:1.

> Eternal life is promised to us, but it is promised to the dead; we are told of the resurrection of the blessed, but meantime we are involved in corruption; we are declared to be just, and sin dwells within us; we hear that we are blessed, but meantime we are overwhelmed by untold miseries; we are promised an abundance of all good things, but we are often hungry and thirsty; God proclaims that He will come to us immediately, but seems to be deaf to our cries. . . . Faith is therefore rightly called the substance of things which are still the objects of hope.[1]

These words of John Calvin in commenting on Hebrews 11:1 were not just theological abstractions for him but reflected the struggles of his own faith. Calvin certainly saw great successes in his life—his writings widely distributed and eagerly read, Reformed churches growing in numbers and influence in many parts of Europe, and a thorough reform of the church in Geneva. Calvin also, however, faced great sorrows and difficulties in his life. He suffered emotionally and spiritually. His wife died after only a few years of marriage, and their only child died in infancy. His stepdaughter was guilty of adultery. Faithful Christians were martyred for the gospel he preached, and some friends apostatized from the faith.

---

[1] John Calvin, *Commentary on Hebrews* (Grand Rapids, MI: Eerdmans, 1974), 157–158.

The struggles of his life tested his faith. At the heart of his faith was the confidence that for the sake of Jesus, God was his loving heavenly Father. But that confidence had to surmount the temptations and sins, the frustrations and losses, the weakness and death that made up so much of his life. He knew that his struggles were the very ones that all God's children faced: "The pious heart, therefore, perceives a division in itself, being partly affected with delight, through a knowledge of God's goodness, partly distressed with sorrow, through a sense of its own calamity; partly relying on the promise of the gospel; partly trembling at the evidence of its own iniquity; partly exulting at the expectation of life; partly alarmed by the fear of death." But faith overcomes that division. With great assurance Calvin declared, "For the invariable issue of this contest is that faith at length overcomes those difficulties, from which, while it is encompassed with them, it appears to be in danger."[2]

Late in his life, as his health deteriorated and his strength ebbed, his friends pled with him to work less diligently, but he refused. By early 1563 he at times was unable to walk due to gout and arthritis. By early 1564 it was clear that his strength was failing seriously. In early February 1564 he gave his last lectures and sermons. Calvin prayed that his mind would remain clear to the end so that he could work. From his bed he continued to dictate letters and his final commentary, on the book of Joshua. His fellow ministers appealed to him to get more rest. He responded, "What! Would you have the Lord find me idle?"[3] He was determined to work hard to the end.

In April he dictated his will, although he did not have much to leave (contrary to the lies his enemies told about his great wealth). He gave expression to his faith in that last testament:

> I give thanks to God, that taking mercy on me, whom he had created and placed in this world, he not only delivered me out of the

---

[2]John Calvin, *Institutes*, III, 2, 18, altered.
[3]Theodore Beza, *The Life of John Calvin*, in *Selected Works of John Calvin*, Vol. 1, ed. H. Beveridge and J. Bonnet (Grand Rapids, MI: Baker, 1983), lxxxiv.

deep darkness of idolatry in which I was plunged, that he might bring me into the light of his gospel, and make me a partaker in the doctrine of salvation, of which I was most unworthy; and not only, with the same mercy and benignity, kindly and graciously bore with my faults and my sins, for which, however, I deserved to be rejected by him and exterminated, but also vouchsafed me such clemency and kindness that he has deigned to use my assistance in preaching and promulgating the truth of his gospel. . . . I have no other defence or refuge for salvation than his gratuitous adoption, on which alone my salvation depends. With my whole soul I embrace the mercy which he has exercised towards me through Jesus Christ, atoning for my sins with the merits of his death and passion, that in this way he might satisfy for all my crimes and faults, and blot them from his remembrance. I testify also and declare, that I suppliantly beg of him that he may be pleased so to wash and purify me in the blood which my Sovereign Redeemer has shed for the sins of the human race, that under his shadow I may be able to stand at the judgment-seat. I likewise declare, that, according to the measure of grace and goodness which the Lord hath employed towards me, I have endeavoured, both in my sermons and also in my writings and commentaries, to preach his Word purely and chastely, and faithfully to interpret his sacred Scriptures. . . . I testify and declare that I trust to no other security for my salvation than this, and this only, viz., that as God is the Father of mercy, he will show himself such a Father to me who acknowledge myself to be a miserable sinner. As to what remains, I wish that, after my departure out of this life, my body be committed to the earth, (after the form and manner which is used in this city,) till the day of a happy resurrection arrive.[4]

His final declaration was a reiteration of the gospel that he had preached and a confession of his own need for the saving work of Christ held out in the gospel.

He said many good-byes in the final weeks of his life. On April 27 the city council came to see him. On April 28 the ministers came to say good-bye. His words to them are somewhat rambling but show what was on his mind:

---

[4]Quoted in ibid., lxxxvi–lxxxvii.

Brethren, after I am dead, persist in this work, and be not dispirited; for the Lord will save this Republic and Church from the threats of the enemy. Let dissension be far away from you, and embrace each other with mutual love. Think again and again what you owe to this Church in which the Lord hath placed you, and let nothing induce you to quit it. It will, indeed, be easy for some who are weary of it to slink away, but they will find, to their experience, that the Lord cannot be deceived. When I first came to this city, the gospel was, indeed, preached, but matters were in the greatest confusion, as if Christianity had consisted in nothing else than the throwing down of images; and there were not a few wicked men from whom I suffered the greatest indignities; but the Lord our God so confirmed me, who am by no means naturally bold, (I say what is true,) that I succumbed to none of their attempts. I afterwards returned thither from Strassburg in obedience to my calling but with an unwilling mind, because I thought I should prove unfruitful. For not knowing what the Lord had determined, I saw nothing before me but numbers of the greatest difficulties. But proceeding in this work, I at length perceived that the Lord had truly blessed my labours. Do you also persist in this vocation, and maintain the established order; at the same time, make it your endeavour to keep the people in obedience to the doctrine; for there are some wicked and contumacious persons. Matters, as you see, are tolerably settled. The more guilty, therefore, will you be before God, if they go to wreck through your indolence. But I declare, brethren, that I have lived with you in the closest bonds of true and sincere affection, and now, in like manner, part from you. But if, while under this disease, you have experienced any degree of peevishness from me, I beg your pardon, and heartily thank you, that when I was sick, you have borne the burden imposed upon you.[5]

On May 2 Calvin, knowing that his death was near, wrote to his old friend William Farel. In fact, Farel, who had insisted that Calvin join him in the work of reforming the church in Geneva in 1538 and brought Calvin into the official ministry, received one of Calvin's last letters. Calvin wrote: "I draw my breath with

---

[5]Quoted in ibid., xciii–xciv.

difficulty, and every moment I am in expectation of breathing my last. It is enough that I live and die for Christ, who is to all his followers a gain in life and in death."[6] Although Calvin urged Farel not to travel for a final visit, Farel, seventy-five and in weak health, made the journey for a personal good-bye.

Beza recorded of Calvin's last days:

> The interval to his death he spent in almost constant prayer. . . . In his sufferings he often groaned like David, "I was silent, O Lord, because thou didst it." . . . I have also heard him say, "You, O Lord crush me; but it is abundantly sufficient for me to know that this is from your hand."[7]

Calvin may also have remembered the words that he had written long ago in his Catechism:

> For death for believers is now nothing but passage to a better life. . . . Hence it follows that death is no longer to be dreaded. We are rather to follow Christ our leader with undaunted mind, who, as he did not perish in death, will not suffer us to perish.[8]

Calvin died peacefully and quietly on Saturday, May 27 at 8 P.M. Beza wrote, "The night and the following day there was a general lamentation throughout the city . . . all lamenting the loss of one who was, under God, a common parent and comforter."[9] The popular image of Calvin today does not think of him as a comforter, but Beza accurately saw that the message of comfort was central to all the pastoral work that Calvin did for the faithful.

He was buried on Sunday in an unmarked grave at a secret location somewhere in Geneva. In one of the last commentaries he wrote, he commented on the death and burial of Moses, "It is good that famous men should be buried in unmarked graves."[10]

---

[6]John Calvin, *Selected Works*, Vol. 7 (Grand Rapids, MI: Baker, 1983), 364.
[7]Beza, *Life of Calvin,* xcv.
[8]"Genevan Catechism," Q. 64–65, 99.
[9]Ibid., xcvi.
[10]John Calvin, *Commentaries on the Four Last Books of Moses,* Vol. 4 (Grand Rapids, MI: Baker, 1979), on Deut. 34:6, 406.

This conviction guided his own burial. He rejected the superstitious veneration of the dead and wanted no pilgrimages to his grave. He had lived to make Christians, not Calvinists. He had perhaps written his own best epitaph in his *Institutes*: ". . . we may patiently pass through this life in afflictions, hunger, cold, contempt, reproaches, and other disagreeable circumstances, contented with this single assurance, that our King will never desert us, but will give what we need, until having finished our warfare, we shall be called to the triumph."[11]

---

[11]Calvin, *Institutes*, II, 15, 4, altered.

General Index

Abraham, 125, 126

Adam, 66, 102, 124, 125, 191

Adoption, spiritual, 84, 114, 123, 160

Affair of the Placards, 30

Apostles' Creed, the, 71, 168

Aquinas, Thomas, 118

Arianism, 45

Artichokes, the, 57

Ascension of Jesus, 41, 99

Athanasius, 74

Atonement, 64, 65, 66

Augsburg Confession, 95

Augustine, 17, 27, 70, 73, 74, 76, 81, 100, 118, 141

authority issues, 19, 20, 30
also see *Scripture, authority of*

baptism, 41, 87, 88, 91, 92, 102, 103, 104, 105, 106, 108, 191
infant baptism, 92, 93, 105, 106, 107, 165

Beza, Theodore, 8, 14, 134, 137, 198

Black Death, the, 62

Bolsec, Jerome, 113, 114, 115, 116, 134

Book of Martyrs (Crespin), 161

Bourgeois, Louis, 75

bubonic plague see *Black Death*

Bucer, Martin, 43, 44, 45, 48, 49, 50, 70, 135, 189

Bude, Guillaume, 152

Bullinger, Heinrich, 39, 96, 98, 115, 147

Calvin, Antoine, 24

Calvin, Charles, 24, 27

Calvin, Gerard, 24, 26, 27

Calvin, Marie, 24

Calvinism, 7, 119, 120, 124, 130, 142
and capitalism, 7
and democracy, 7
and science, 7

Caroli, Pierre, 45

Charles V, Emperor, 48, 77

Christmas, 41

Chrysostom, 70, 74

Church, the, 80, 101, 107, 163, 169, 188, 189
   authority of, 30, 39, 179
   church discipline, 39, 40, 41, 59, 118, 134 also see *excommunication*
   reform of, 22, 29, 30, 39, 48, 77
   and state, 38, 39, 40, 41, 59, 129, 130, 167
   unity of, 20, 48, 49, 162, 166, 197
   and Word of God, 21, 176, 179

Cicero, 171, 185

Circumcision, 92, 103, 104, 105

Clauburger, John, 164, 165

Communion, 41, 44, 48, 49, 59, 70, 71, 72, 81, 82, 88, 89, 90, 91, 93, 94, 95, 96, 98, 99, 102, 105, 106, 107, 108, 109, 110, 161

confirmation, 88

conscience, 16, 17, 18, 19, 51, 53, 81, 85, 101, 170, 180

Consensus, the see *Zurich Consensus or Agreement*

Consensus Tigurinus see *Zurich Consensus or Agreement*

Constantine, Emperor, 129

Contarini, Cardinal, 49

Covenants, the, 124, 125, 126

covenant of grace, 124, 125, 127

covenant of works, 124, 125

two-covenant theology, 124

Crespin, Jean, 161

David, King, 28, 73, 143, 149, 150, 179, 198

death, 18, 63, 65, 140, 147, 151, 198

de Bude, Madame, 152

de Bure (Calvin), Idolette, 46, 47

de Coligny, Madame, 147

De Clementia (Seneca), 27

de Hangest family, 25

Depravity of man, 17, 125

Devil, the see *Satan*

"Draft Ecclesiastical Ordinances," 58

Duke of Guise, 149, 150

Dukes of Savoy, 36

Durant, Will, 8

Easter, 41

Eck, John, 109

education, Christian, 38, 44, 67, 106, 135, 136, 137

election, the elect, 104, 114, 115, 116, 117, 118, 119, 120, 121, 122, 123, 124, 125, 126, 127, 146, 151

Erasmus, Desiderius, 27

Esau, 122

Eucharist, the, 88, 89, 90, 95, 102, 107, 108, 109, 110
excommunication, 39, 40, 59, 70, 134
expiation, 99
extreme unction, 88

faith, 19, 20, 31, 32, 33, 39, 51, 52, 53, 81, 82, 84, 85, 87, 89, 91, 92, 93, 94, 96, 99, 100, 101, 102, 103, 104, 106, 107, 110, 114, 116, 117, 121, 139, 145, 146, 147, 152, 153, 156, 157, 160, 162, 167, 168, 169, 175, 177, 182, 183, 186, 188, 189, 194, 195
faithfulness, 20, 51, 67, 72, 77, 85, 87, 91, 93, 125, 141, 145, 152, 153, 156, 157, 179, 187, 190
Fall, the, 79
Farel, William (Guillaume), 8, 36, 37, 38, 42, 44, 47, 49, 57, 58, 61, 96, 114, 115, 197, 198
fatalism, 113, 141, 142
fear of God, 84, 85, 106, 121, 154, 155, 186
flesh, the, 79, 82, 85, 92, 126, 144, 154, 159, 192
forgiveness of sins, 32, 63, 64, 65, 66, 91, 92, 103, 108
Form of Prayers and Manner of Ministering the Sacra-
ments according to the Use of the Ancient Church, 69, 72
Fourth Lateran Council, 89
Free will, 89, 116, 117

Genevan Catechism, 60, 87, 90, 101, 186, 193, 198
Genevan Confession, 38
Genevan Psalter, 69, 70, 75, 76
gospel, the, 21, 22, 32, 40, 49, 51, 52, 53, 75, 91, 117, 121, 131, 135, 149, 151, 157, 159, 177, 178, 183, 189, 196
grace, 22, 32, 51, 52, 63, 64, 85, 86, 88, 89, 90, 91, 93, 96, 97, 104, 117, 118, 120, 123, 124, 154, 159, 160, 187, 192, 196
Greek thought, writings, 23, 26, 27
Gruet, Jacques, 130
Guillermins, the, 57

heaven, 82, 83, 94, 99, 144, 155, 192
Heresy, 39, 89, 131, 133, 134
holy orders, 88
Holy Roman Empire, 35
hope, 18, 19, 93, 172, 175, 194
Humanism, humanist writings, 27

Idolatry, 79, 83, 90, 108, 132, 152, 153, 196

imputation of Christ's righteousness, 19, 32, 52, 63

Innocent III, Pope, 89

Inquisition, the, 39

Institutes of Oratory (Quintilian), 15

Institutes of the Christian Religion (Calvin), 13, 17, 31, 33, 37, 50, 51, 77, 87, 94, 101, 115, 118, 133, 139, 140, 142, 146, 167, 168, 169, 170, 176, 179, 184, 185, 186, 187, 192, 199

Isaac, 122

Isaiah, the prophet, 179

Jacob, 122

James, the apostle, 53

Jerome, 27

John, the apostle, 150

joy, 75, 84, 85, 145, 161

Judas, 122

justification, 16, 18, 19, 21, 31, 49, 52, 53, 100, 102, 114, 191

kingdom of God, 32, 49, 123, 148, 151, 182, 187, 192

Latin thought, writings, 27

Law of God, 32, 52, 53, 66, 75, 106, 125, 149, 167, 168, 177, 178, 189, 190, 191

Le Franc, Jeanne, 24

Liner, John, 159

Lord's Supper see *Communion*

Louis XII, King, 148

Luther, Martin, 27, 29, 43, 46, 48, 49, 51, 90, 95, 99, 100, 118, 170

marriage, sacrament of, 88

martyrdom, 157, 161, 180, 194

Mass, the, 102, 108, 109, 152

Melanchthon, Philipp, 48, 49, 50, 95, 117, 118

Middle Ages, the, 39, 46, 89, 130, 135

Moses, 198

Music see *worship, music in*

New Covenant, the, 74, 75, 81, 102, 104, 149

Nicene Creed, the, 45

Ninety-five Theses of Luther, 43

Olbrac, William, 163

Old Covenant, the, 81, 104

"On the Necessity of Reforming the Church" (Calvin), 77

ordination see *holy orders*

original sin, 102, 103

passover, the, 105
Paul, the apostle, 53, 64, 65, 66, 74, 118, 119, 121, 122, 125, 126, 191
penance, 88, 110
Pentecost, 41
persecution, persecuted believers, 151, 152, 153, 154, 156, 157, 159, 160, 194
perseverance of the saints, 124, 144, 151
Peter, the apostle, 65, 123
Plato, 76
Poulain, Valeran, 162, 163, 165, 166
prayer, 31, 70, 72, 73, 100, 143, 145, 146, 151, 154, 160, 190, 198
predestination, 113, 114, 115, 116, 117, 118, 119, 120, 121, 123, 126, 127, 139, 140, 146
double predestination, 122
promises of God, 19, 31, 32, 70, 87, 90, 91, 92, 93, 96, 100, 101, 102, 103, 104, 117, 118, 125, 126, 141, 145, 155, 157, 158, 160, 183, 189, 190, 194
providence, 139, 140, 141, 142, 143, 144, 145, 146, 148, 157, 166

Quintilian, 15

Rebekah, 122
reconciliation with God, 32, 62, 64, 65, 93, 97, 192
redemption, 32, 63, 64, 93, 94, 97, 102, 124, 125, 127, 160, 169, 171, 187, 191, 192, 196
Reformation, the, 14, 17, 20, 22, 27, 29, 43, 46, 50, 57, 77, 87, 89, 90, 129, 131, 135, 184
German Reformation, 48
Reformed Christianity, theology, 7, 9, 14, 31, 86, 124, 125, 130, 156, 161, 166, 186, 190
Reformers, the, 29, 39, 46, 48, 88, 90, 129, 184, 188
regeneration, 52, 61, 104, 106
Renaissance, the, 23, 26, 27, 135, 152
Renee of France, Duchess, 30, 148, 149, 150
repentance, 85, 92, 94, 100, 110
"Reply to Sadoleto" (Calvin), 14, 15, 16, 17, 21, 22, 30, 50, 77, 180
Reprobation, the reprobate, 121, 122, 150, 151
Restitution of the Christian Religion (Servetus), 133
resurrection, 169, 194, 196
of Christ, 124, 192

revelation by God, 53, 115, 116, 172, 173, 174, 175, 177, 178, 179, 186, 188, 189

Roman thought, writings, 23, 26

Sadoleto, Jacopo, 14, 15, 16, 18, 19, 20, 21, 22, 174, 175

sacraments, the, 31, 81, 82, 83, 87, 88, 89, 90, 91, 92, 93, 94, 95, 96, 97, 98, 99, 100, 101, 102, 103, 104, 105, 106, 107, 108, 109, 110, 111, 162, 167, 169

salvation, 16, 18, 19, 32, 61, 65, 67, 77, 78, 95, 97, 100, 104, 116, 117, 118, 120, 121, 123, 125, 126, 127, 140, 148, 158, 165, 170, 175, 177, 186, 188, 189, 192, 196

sanctification, 32, 51, 52, 53, 103, 110

Satan, 63, 65, 79, 122, 155, 161, 174

Scripture, 31, 32, 53, 67, 69, 71, 72, 78, 79, 80, 81, 83, 85, 86, 87, 89, 91, 93, 98, 119, 120, 127, 155, 159, 169, 170, 173, 174, 175, 176, 177, 178, 179, 180, 181, 182, 183, 184, 185, 186, 187, 188, 196

authority of, 20, 21, 30, 170, 180, 182, 183, 184

interpretation of, 169, 177, 178, 184

reliability of, 31, 170, 174, 176, 186

sufficiency of, 170, 176, 177, 179

unity through, 21

second Adam, the (Christ), 124–125, 191

"Second Defense" (Calvin), 100

Servetus, Michael, 132, 133, 134

"Short Treatise on the Holy Supper of Our Lord" (Calvin), 94

sola Scriptura, 20

Seneca, 15, 27, 29

sin, consequences of and dealing with, 16, 17, 18, 19, 64, 65, 78, 79, 86, 102, 110, 116, 124, 168, 172, 194

Sovereignty of God, 60, 86, 120, 121, 140, 141, 142, 157

Stoics, the, 84

Sturm, Johannes, 44

suffering, 143, 152, 154, 156

Tradition, 89, 169, 173, 176, 177

Transubstantiation, 49, 89, 90, 95, 107, 108, 109
Trinity, the, 132, 133
Trolliet, John, 117, 118

unbelief, 98, 122, 183

Valla, Lorenzo, 115
Vauville, Richard, 148, 162
Viret, Pierre, 47

Warfield, B. B., 168
Westphal, Joachim, 100
wisdom, 17, 69, 144, 170
Word of God see *Scripture*
works, 19, 53, 65, 89, 124
worship, 69, 70, 71, 72, 73, 75, 77, 78, 79, 80, 81, 82, 83, 84, 85, 86, 88, 89, 100, 108, 131, 143, 144, 152, 157, 172, 177
    music in, 73, 74, 75, 76
    regulative principle of, 78

wrath of God, 64, 65, 122, 124

zeal for God, 16, 76, 78, 149, 163
Zechariah (Zacharias), song of, 65
Zurich Consensus or Agreement, 96, 97, 98, 99
Zwingli, Ulrich, 43, 90, 95, 96, 97, 118